EDITOR: MARTIN WINDROW

 MEN-AT-ARMS SERIES [148]

THE ARMY OF ALEXANDER THE GREAT

Text by
NICK SEKUNDA
Colour plates by
ANGUS McBRIDE

First published in Great Britain in 1984 by
Osprey, a division of Reed Consumer Books Limited
Michelin House, 81 Fulham Road, London SW3 6RB
© Copyright 1984 Reed International Books Limited
Reprinted 1985, 1986, 1987 (twice), 1988, 1989, 1992,
1993, 1994, 1995 (twice), 1996, 1997

British Library Cataloguing in Publication Data
Sekunda, N.
    The Army of Alexander the Great.—(Men-at-Arms series;
    148)
    1. Macedonia—Armies—History
    I. Title   II. Series
    355'.00938'07   U33

    ISBN 0-85045-539-1

Filmset in Great Britain
Printed through World Print Ltd, Hong Kong

The Army of Alexander the Great

Introduction

The figures of Napoleon and Alexander stand comparison: both were supremely successful generals, both were short of stature, both dreamed of world conquest, both covered up their failures, and both came to be virtually worshipped. The same comparison cannot be made of the modern literature dealing with their armies. There are books dealing with Alexander's principal battles and campaigns, books dealing with his generalship and with limited aspects of the army, but no book dealing with the army as such.

The reasons for this are not hard to find. We only know the details of Alexander's reign from a small number of works written some centuries after the events they describe. These frequently contradict one another, and in many cases they can be shown to contain obvious errors. The patient work of scores of scholars over the last century has advanced our knowledge of the details of the Macedonian army immeasurably and, although many problems still defy solution, we have perhaps reached a position now where such a book can be attempted.

A monograph of this size cannot pretend to fill the gap. Almost every statement in the text below could be challenged. Lack of space has made it impossible to credit the work of previous scholars and the individual suggestions they have made to resolve particular problems; but it is hoped that the debate can be followed through the pages of the books mentioned under 'Further Reading'. Conversely, some new suggestions have been advanced in the text, but again lack of space has prevented me from defending them in full detail. I have also limited my subject to the army down to the end of 331 BC, though I have dealt with the later reforms in outline, and I have continued some of the unit histories beyond that date. So while this book does not attempt a comprehensive treatment, it is offered as an introduction to Alexander's army.

What brings the events of 2,300 years ago to life more than anything else is the vivid picture we create in our mind's eye of the glorious struggle described in the texts, so this book concentrates on giving an idea of how the regiments of the army were uniformed. Two archaeological sources are of inestimable value. The Alexander Mosaic is a Roman copy of a contemporary painting, possibly an apotheosis-painting of Alexander in battle against the Persians by Apelles. Colour reproductions occur in most illustrated books on Alexander. The Alexander Sarcophagus, commissioned by Alexander's vassal King Abdalonymus of Sidon and now in the Archaeological Museum, Istanbul, is not so accessible to the general reader. The once-vivid paint which originally adorned the figures was already greatly faded when the

A gold medallion showing the head of Philip of Macedon, from a hoard of such pieces, featuring various members of the royal house, dating from the Roman period—mid-3rd century AD—and recovered at Tarsus in the last century. Recent reconstruction from the partially cremated skull found in Philip's tomb at Vergina demonstrated that his right eye had been destroyed, with massive tissue damage to the socket. Ancient sources tell us that the king's eye was shot out during the siege of Methone. (Bibliothèque Nationale, Paris)

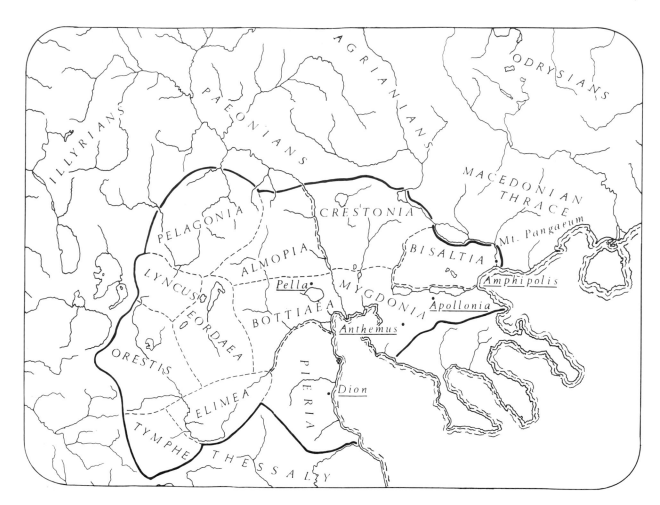

sarcophagus was excavated nearly a century ago. The paint faded rapidly on excavation and progressively thereafter. The original publication of O. Hamdy Bey and Theodore Reinach—*Une nécropole royale à Sidon* (Paris 1892)—included some heliochromes of the Sarcophagus which, despite their generally poor quality, add some details to the magnificently complete *Der Alexandersarkophag aus Sidon* (Strassburg 1912) of F. Winter. Both these books are extremely rare, and can only be found in a very few libraries in this country. Some further information can be gleaned from G. Mendel's Catalogue of Sculptures in the Museum (although this information has to be treated with some caution); and from Volkmar von Graeve's *Der Alexandersarkophag und seine Werkstatt* (Berlin 1970), which uses special photography to add details of the faded paint not now visible, and is most useful for its complete notes. Finally, some problems of contradictory information have been resolved (and some guesses made) from personal observations made in Istanbul, and I would like to take this opportunity to thank the Museum authorities and friends in Istanbul for their help and time given under difficult circumstances.

Philip's Army

When Philip II ascended the throne at the age of 23 in 359 BC, Macedonia was in danger of being engulfed by wild barbarian tribes to the north and wily Greek cities to the south. They exploited her internal weaknesses: there were other pretenders to the throne, and authority could be exerted over the semi-independent principalities of Upper Macedonia only intermittently. Philip had to expand the power of the throne or be swallowed up by the difficulties surrounding him: the creation of a powerful army was imperative.

Philip dealt with the northern tribes first. Like his

own army, these tribal levies were but lightly equipped—peltasts armed with javelins and light shields (*peltai*). Philip re-armed his infantry, composed of peasant levies—all healthy male subjects of the king were liable for service—with longer, heavier fighting spears; and issued them with some light armour, borrowing the ideas of the Athenian general Iphicrates, who had been campaigning in the area shortly beforehand. This new force of infantry was toughened up by long training marches under the summer sun, and mercenary generals were brought in to impose discipline and instruct in drill. The northern tribesmen were dealt with by this improvised force of infantry; but a showdown with the armies of Greece was inevitable, and his infantry needed to be much better equipped to stand up to the Greek hoplites.

Greek battles had been decided up to now by the manoeuvres of heavy infantry, the hoplites, who had become increasingly lightly equipped during the 4th century, abandoning much of their armour. This enabled them to execute their tactical evolutions on the battlefield with speed and without too much fatigue.

Philip, however, created a large force of heavily-equipped cavalry to act as the *corps de rupture* of his army. At first he had only about 600 Companion cavalrymen. Noble families from all over the Greek world were settled on fiefs created out of lands won from the king's enemies, and by the end of his reign their number had been multiplied many times over. Philip gave them heavy armour—cuirasses and helmets of the 'Phrygian' type—and he further developed the new tactical formations Jason of Pherai had invented to enable his cavalry to take a leading role in battle. The infantry no longer needed its mobility.

Philip consolidated his hold on the rich mines of Pangaeum, which yielded 1,000 talents annually, and re-equipped his infantry with the bronze hoplite shields and cuirasses which had been abandoned in the rest of Greece for more than half a century. Thus, when the final showdown came in 338 BC at Chaeronea, the Greek hoplites smashed themselves to pieces against the solid lines of the more heavily-equipped Macedonian phalanx. An unwilling Greece was united under Philip in the League of Corinth; but the king was assassinated at

A relief from Pelinna in Thessaly: the cloak identifies this horseman as a Macedonian, while the 'Phrygian' helmet is very similar to that found in the Vergina tomb. The artist has omitted reins, horse-furniture and boots. Note that the rider is shown clean-shaven. (Louvre, Paris)

the age of 46 before he could launch his planned expedition against the Persian Empire.

The first year of Alexander's reign was taken up in re-establishing his hold on Greece and the Balkans, but he found time to introduce some changes in the army. He introduced stave-fighting into the training programme, and in the cavalry he replaced the 'Phrygian' helmet with the Boeotian, which gave more protection to the face and shoulders against sword-cuts. He also ordered the army to shave, officially to deny the enemy a hand-hold in close combat. Shaving was only just becoming popular in Greece and many of the older members of the court refused to rid themselves of their curly beards. Looking at busts of the new king, who had just turned 20, one wonders if he had any need to obey the regulation himself.

PRINCIPAL DATES IN THE REIGNS OF PHILIP AND ALEXANDER

359	Philip becomes king.
356	Alexander born.
338	?2 August: Battle of Chaeronea.
336	Spring: Expeditionary force sent to Asia, withdrawn on death of Philip(?)
	Summer: Alexander becomes king.

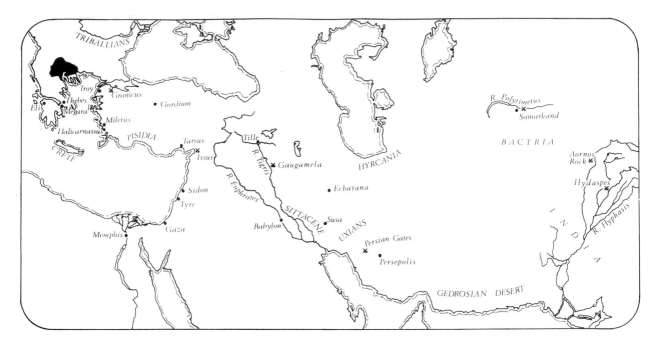

335	Spring: Balkan Campaigns.
	Destruction of Thebes.
334	Spring: Expeditionary force crosses Hellespont.
	May: Battle of Granicus.
	Sieges of Miletus and Halicarnassus.
334/3	Winter campaign in Pisidia.
333	Reinforcements reach army at Gordium.
	September/October: Battle of Issus.
332	Siege of Tyre.
	Siege of Gaza.
332/1	Reinforcements reach army in Memphis and Syria.
331	?30 September: Battle of Gaugamela.
	?November: Army re-forms in Sittacene.
	Campaign against the Uxians.
330	Late January: Storming of Persian Gates.
	?June–July: Greek allies dismissed at Ecbatana; pursuit of Darius.
	Hyrcanian Campaign.
329	Operations near Samarkand; massacre at the River Polytimetus.
327/6	Capture of Aornos Rock.
326	Indian campaign begins.
	Battle of Hydaspes.
	Mutiny on the Hyphasis.
325	March through Gedrosian Desert.
323	10/11 June: Alexander dies.

The Court

The army, like the state, was run from the court which always travelled with the king. This comprised a hundred or so courtiers, called 'Personal Companions' (*hoi amph' auton hetairoi*) or sometimes simply 'Companions' (*hetairoi*) in the texts. These Companions should not be confused with the Companion Cavalry; 'Companion' is simply a court title. Thus when we hear of a Companion being appointed to command such-and-such a unit, the man in question should be considered a Personal Companion. Similarly, when we hear of Alexander addressing a council of Companions we should understand that the young king has assembled a small group of his courtiers, not a democratic assembly of the Companion Cavalry. Our sources also refer to the king's 'Friends' (*philoi*), a term for courtier current in Hellenistic times. It could refer to the highest grade of Personal Companion at court, but it could also be an anachronism, simply equating with Personal Companion. In battle the Personal Companions fought alongside the king in the Royal Squadron of the Companion Cavalry.

One figure on the Alexander Sarcophagus wears a purple Macedonian cloak with a yellow border (see Plate B3). In Hellenistic times the king would give his courtiers purple cloaks as a mark of their rank, so it seems that the practice was already established in Alexander's reign, the figure representing a Personal Companion. After the battle of Issus, Alexander sends Leonnatus to inform the Persian royal family that Darius has not died; Diodorus describes Leonnatus as one of the Friends while Curtius terms him *ex purpuratis*. Alexander sometimes wore 'fancy dress' in his battles, but he normally dressed in the uniform of an officer of the Companion Cavalry. He is dressed as such on the Alexander Mosaic (see Plate A1), but he wears the purple cloak of a Personal Companion and not the regimental cloak. The edge of the cloak is destroyed on the mosaic, but the border is clearly shown on some of the bronze statuettes representing Alexander. Our sources mention the royal trappings worn by the king's horse; perhaps these may be the elaborate metal harness ornaments shown on the mosaic.

The king ran the army from the royal tent. This seems to have been an impressive pavilion, with a large chamber where the council of war met (perhaps separate from the main tent); a vestibule beyond, which none could enter without passing Chares the royal usher (*eisangeleus*); the armoury (perhaps also separate from the main tent); and the king's apartments, in which he bathed, and slept, beyond the vestibule. It was court custom for all to remove their headdress when addressing the king. The tent was dug in and erected by its own work-party, commanded by a Macedonian called Proxenus. The person of the king was ministered to by his chamberlains (*rhabdophoroi, rhabdouchoi*), or 'wand-carriers', the wand being their badge of office. These men accompanied the king when bathing, dressing, etc., and were selected both for their wit and their fidelity. The royal tent itself was guarded by a watch selected from the Bodyguards (*sōmatophylakes*) on a rota basis, while the area of the royal quarters was defended by a detachment of Hypaspists.

No Greek army was complete without a 'chaplains' department', whose job it was to provide favourable omens by augury to satisfy the suspicious soldiery. Aristander the seer performed this role with considerable aplomb, but on occasion even Aristander needed a little help. A passage in Frontinus describes how Alexander, a self-styled divinity himself, used a special preparation to write 'victory is ordained for Alexander' on Aristander's hand before a sacrifice. During the ceremony the

This head of Alexander, originally from Alexandria and now in the British Museum, shows the young king at the age of 20—we are reminded that he ordered his army to shave off facial hair. (British Museum)

priest would put his hand under the victim's innards, and it would magically acquire the divine message to be shown to the gawping army. At the battle of Gaugamela an eagle was observed flying over the king. Our sources describe Aristander's dress, as he rode along the Macedonian line pointing out the omen, as consisting of white robes with a golden crown on his head (which we should understand to be a wreath of leaves worked in gold) and a laurel wreath in his right hand. Sacrificial knives took the shape of a small *kopis*.

The Royal Pages

It was a practice going back to Philip's time that the sons of the Macedonian nobility who had reached adolescence should be enrolled into the Royal Pages (*basilikoi paides*). At court these young men received

Roman bronze of Alexander: note the border shown on the king's cloak. (British Museum)

their education, and at the same time they served as a guarantee of their parents' loyalty. (Should any Macedonian be found guilty of treason, the custom was that the whole family involved should be wiped out root and branch.) No one had the power of chastising them by flogging except the king himself. The noble youths were given a general education in philosophy and the other liberal disciplines, but an emphasis was put on the more manly pursuits of hunting and *sphaira*—a violent ball game similar to rugby football.

The most important role of the institution, however, was to inculcate obedience to the king and deference to the king's majesty into the noble youth of Macedonia. Consequently they were called upon to perform duties not very different from those of slaves. They served on the king at table, stood guard at the doors of his bed-chamber and led in his concubines, poured the king's bath, prepared his dinner, and under the supervision of the royal chamberlains they performed all the menial functions required by the royal household.

They also accompanied the king out of doors. They received the horses from the grooms, led them up to the king and helped him mount. They may also have performed similar functions for the king's Personal Companions. We hear of an official called the 'Royal Groom' who seems to be a senior member of the Court entrusted with the care of the king's horses. They also looked after the king's armour, and accompanied him in the hunt.

Two mosaics from Pella show young men of the court at the hunt. They wear a narrow rectangular white cloak fastened with a brooch. In two cases the cloak has a red border and two of the young men wear white sun-hats: these are probably Royal Pages.

On leaving the Royal Pages the young men would either be trained as officers in the Royal Bodyguard, if they had proved themselves able, or they would enter the ranks of the aristocratic Companion Cavalry regiment.

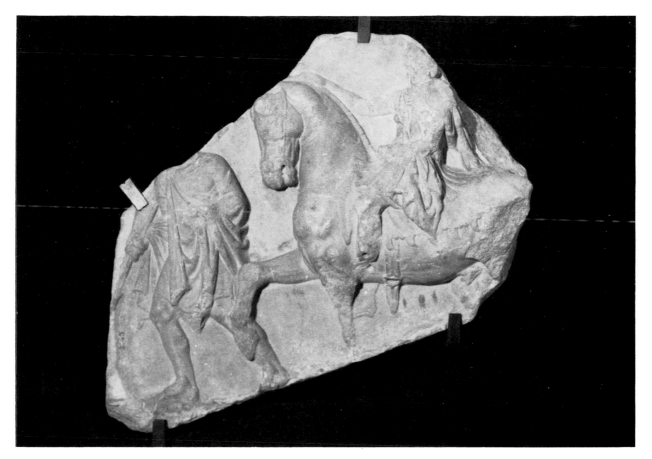

The Bodyguards

Our sources frequently mention a Bodyguard (*sōmatophylakia*) or Bodyguards (*sōmatophylakes*); in Curtius they are called *armigeri* or *satellites*. These men are generally assumed to be a detachment of the Hypaspists detailed to guard the king. This is improbable, however, for in three separate passages (3.17.2, 4.3.2, 4.30.3) Arrian mentions that Alexander takes with him the Bodyguards *and* the Hypaspists. So it seems that the Bodyguard is a separate unit—and a unit of some strength, for in the third passage Arrian speaks of some 700 Bodyguards and Hypaspists. If we were to deduct a *lochos* of Hypaspists we would be left with a number of 200 or so for the Bodyguard. Nor was the unit one of insignificant status, for Alexander's close friend Hephaistion, who was appointed a brigadier in the Companion Cavalry in 330, commanded the Bodyguard at Gaugamela only a year earlier (Diodorus 17.61.3).

The most senior rank in the army was that of 'Royal Bodyguard' (*sōmatophylax basilikos*), the equivalent of *archisōmatophylax* in Hellenistic armies,

A relief from Troy showing Alexander: the horse-furniture has several interesting features, such as the buckle on the saddle girth. Note the figure on the left. The object held in the right hand does not seem to be a spear, since it is carried under the right arm: it could be a chamberlain's wand of office. (Museo Arqueologico Nacional, Madrid)

or of 'staff officer' in more modern armies. There were seven Royal Bodyguards, and this number was rigidly maintained. If a Royal Bodyguard were made satrap or died, another general was immediately promoted to take his place. The number seven was probably connected with the Bodyguards' original function of providing a daily watch to guard the king's tent. When Peucestas saved the king's life in India the number of Royal Bodyguards was changed to eight, as Alexander wanted to appoint him instantly as a mark of his gratitude. We frequently hear of a Royal Bodyguard being appointed to temporary command of a division of the army.

The Bodyguard itself seems to have been composed of young adult noblemen, for Diodorus (17.65.1) mentions that the army, when in Sittacene, was joined by 50 sons of the king's friends

9

sent by their fathers to serve as bodyguards. The equivalent passage in Curtius is rather confused, for he adds that the fifty sons were adults, but he then goes on to describe the duties of the Royal Pages—which these men would not perform if they were adult. Indeed, the man who brought this detachment from Macedonia, Amyntas son of Andromenes, later states, during his trial, that Alexander had sent him to Macedonia to fetch the 'many young men fit for service who were hidden away in your mother's palace'—so it seems that the 50 had already served as Royal Pages in Macedonia.

The Bodyguard, then, seems to have been composed of young men who had already served in the Royal Pages. They acted as personal bodyguards to the king and guarded his tent, but the Bodyguard probably also combined the functions of an officer training corps and a staff corps. They may have acted as aides to the Royal Bodyguards, but even if this were not the case they would certainly be at the centre of things and so would gain a good idea of how the army worked. I believe it is highly probable that the Macedonian officer corps had all seen service in the Bodyguard at one time or another. As we have already seen, however, from time to time the Bodyguard was called upon to fight as an active unit, so the young men would also gain some practical experience of soldiering.

The Bodyguards seem to be distinguished by a distinctive uniform, for Amyntas is allowed to wear the dress of a Bodyguard during his trial. Unfortunately no further details are given (though see Plates E2, E3 and H2), but the Bodyguards do seem to use javelins in some places in the texts.

Command and Communications

The army Alexander took over to Asia in the spring of 334 BC was far from homogeneous. Its core was the army of the Kingdom of Macedonia itself, hereafter called the 'Royal Army'. Added to this were contingents supplied to the expeditionary force by the vassal princedoms on Macedonia's borders—Paeonians, Agrianians, Triballians, Odrysians and Illyrians. Alexander was also *archon* of

The mosaics of the royal palace at Pella frequently depict young men of the court, probably Royal Pages, in hunting scenes. They wear small cloaks, either white or white with red borders. (Pella Museum)

Trumpeter in the dress of a Thessalian cavalryman, drawn from a 5th century Corinthian vase in the National Museum, Athens.

Thessaly and so head of the Thessalian army. He was also head of the League of Corinth, which most of the states of Greece had been forced to join, and which supplied Alexander with contingents of infantry, cavalry and ships from their own armed forces. Finally, the numbers of the expeditionary force were augmented by a large number of mercenaries who were mostly Greeks, though some of Alexander's units of Balkan troops may have been mercenaries too.

The Greeks could not understand the strange patois of their language spoken by the Macedonians, and did not consider them to be Greek at all. To the Greeks they were uncouth, semi-civilised barbarians. The Macedonians for their part despised the Greeks as éffete, wishy-washy Greeklings. Both regarded the Thracians as scarcely capable of walking on their hind legs. It is a tribute to the leadership of the army that racial tensions were kept at such a low key. King Philip had once

Two examples of a rare silver *dekadrachm* showing Alexander in battle with Porus' elephants. The reverse shows Victory about to crown Alexander, who holds a thunderbolt. Both coins are very worn; but Alexander seems to wear a cuirass, a plumed and crested helmet of 'Phrygian' shape, and a peculiar type of cloak—perhaps an *ephaptis*? The king may be in the uniform of a senior officer of the Bodyguards. The lappets showing underneath the helmet may belong to a helmet liner: cf. Plate D1. (British Museum)

been wounded in rioting between his Macedonian soldiers and Greek mercenaries, and had only been able to escape by feigning death.

At its highest level the army was commanded by its staff officers, the 'Royal Bodyguards', and by the other generals (*stratēgoi*). The army would frequently be divided into a number of divisions (*moirai*), especially during the later campaigns, and a general would be appointed to command each. It was usual for these generals to retain direct command of an individual unit too, so many of the infantry *taxeis* were commanded by *stratēgoi*, not *taxiarchs*. Below the generals were the rest of the officers, the *hēgemones*, who were selected from the families of the Macedonian aristocracy. The officers were allowed their own baggage animals and servants and many, it seems, maintained their own 'train'. Command of individual units was very much a family affair. Many of the army units seem to be commanded by members of baronial families prominent in the area where they had been recruited. Perdiccas son of Orontes, who commands the *taxis* from Orestis, was of royal stock, probably from the ducal house of Orestis. The *taxis* of Amyntas son of Andromenes was commanded by his brother Simmias when Amyntas was back in Macedonia recruiting more troops, and another brother, Attalus, may have taken over command of the *taxis* after Amyntas' death. The Macedonian peasantry had to be commanded by men it respected. The 'new men' Philip had admitted into the ranks of the Companions were scarcely less noble, though not of vintage Macedonian stock. These men had to make do with less prestigious army commands. Thus we find the two sons of Larichus of Mitylene, Erigyius and Laomedon, both favourites of Alexander, making do with a brigade of Allied Horse and a commission in charge of the barbarian captives respectively.

Command was very centralised. The king himself would give the army its orders, down to such details as when to take breakfast. At first these were all given by trumpet signals. We hear of trumpet signals for the attack, the withdrawal, the call to arms, strike camp, march, ground arms and the alarm. The signal would be given first of all by Alexander's trumpeter, and then taken up by the trumpeters attached to each unit. It may be that at the lower levels the regimental trumpeters added a unit prefix to their trumpet signals, as is the case in modern armies. The day and the night were both divided into a number of watches, and it seems that the change of watch was signalled by trumpet, although this may be a detail of Roman military practice inserted into his narrative by Curtius. Similarly the frequent references to standards in Curtius are to be rejected as a Roman embellishment of the text.

Administration

The whole of Alexander's empire was run by a secretariat divided up into various sections (e.g. the Treasury), each, it seems, run by a Royal Secretary (*grammateus basilikos*). We can compare the 'Royal' Secretaries to the 'Royal' Bodyguards—both officers of the highest rank in the secretariat and the army. The Army Secretariat was under Eumenes of Cardia, who rose to prominence as one of the ablest of the warlords who disputed Alexander's empire after his death. Eumenes is once described as *archigrammateus* (chief secretary), but the title has a Hellenistic ring about it and it may be anachronistic.

The men who made up the Secretariat, though they might be able and even Personal Companions of the king, were usually men debarred by obscurity of birth or physical infirmity from holding a field command. These 'basest of men' were despised by the officers of the rest of the army. After Alexander's death Neoptolemus, the commander of the Hypaspists, was heard to remark that he had followed the king with his spear and shield, but Eumenes only with his escritoir.

The Army Secretariat was based in the tent of the Royal Secretary of the Army, which contained copies of all correspondence relevant to the army and all army documentation. The bases of army documentation were the muster-rolls (*syllogismous*) and conduct sheets (*syntelesas*), which gave the current strengths of the various units, and according to which pay and equipment, reinforcements, and on occasion rations were distributed and promotions were made. We hear of arms, armour, clothing, goblets and baggage-animals being issued in this way, on an occasional general issue basis rather than on a permanent one-for-one basis. Thus we should conclude that stores were not held at unit level but were held centrally in the baggage train.

When stores were distributed this was done by *lochoi* in the infantry and *ilai* in the cavalry (*hekatostuas* or 'hundreds' after 331). At company and squadron level it was then the duty of the *hypēretai*, or 'attendants', to allocate the stores further. We hear of these *hypēretai* only once in Diodorus (17.109.2), when the ringleaders of a mutiny are handed over to them for punishment. In Hellenistic times the *hypēretai* performed the duties of a modern sergeant-major. Responsible for matters concerning discipline and administration, he would maintain the muster-rolls and conduct sheets, and, in general, help the *lochagos* or *ilarch* run his command. Promoted from the ranks, we may imagine that his ultimate aspiration was to 'fly a desk' in the Army Secretariat.

The Army Secretariat was divided into various sections, each under a Secretary (*grammateus*) assisted by a number of Inspectors (*episkopoi*). We hear of a Secretary of Cavalry and a Secretary of Mercenaries for Egypt, who has two Inspectors under him. We also hear of Inspectors being detached from the main army to administer the military forces left in a province. The Secretary of Cavalry had the most difficult job, as one of his responsibilities was the procurement and distribution of remounts. Huge numbers of horses died in battle, and in an age before horseshoes a cavalry mount could easily be ruined by a long march. At the battle of Gaugamela the cavalry, 7,000 strong, lost a thousand mounts: nearly one in three of the Companion Cavalry lost theirs. Sequestration was used to obtain remounts locally, but more usually it was the duty of provincial governors to procure horses and despatch them to the remount pool. Many cities or provinces paid tribute on the hoof. In the last resort recourse had to be made to sequestration of surplus mounts within the army itself. We hear of an argument between the powerful nobleman Amyntas son of Andromenes

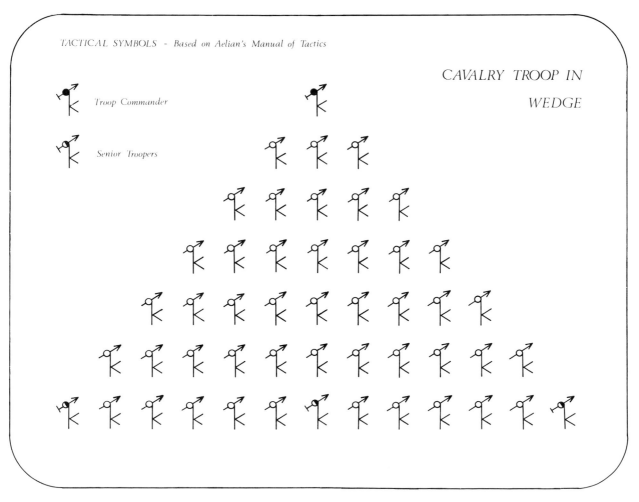

TACTICAL SYMBOLS - *Based on Aelian's Manual of Tactics*

CAVALRY TROOP IN WEDGE

Troop Commander

Senior Troopers

and Antiphanes the Secretary of Horse. Amyntas complains that Antiphanes, 'the basest of men', has taken eight out of the 10 horses he brought with him from Macedonia.

Rations were not generally issued. It was the responsibility of each soldier to purchase his own rations from the host of sutlers, frequently Phoenician traders, who followed the army. The local inhabitants of conquered territory were often obliged to provide markets for the soldiery when provisions were scarce. Sequestration was used in the last resort. If the army was about to cross barren areas, however, where the normal system would break down, rations were collected and held centrally in the baggage train, sealed with the Royal Seal, ready for emergency distribution.

The Cavalry

Organisation and Tactics

The building-block of the cavalry was the *ilē* (squadron) of 200 men, commanded by an *ilarch* and divided into four *tetrarchiai* of 49 men, each under the command of a *tetrarch*. The tactical formation adopted by the *tetrarchia* was the 'wedge', an invention of Philip, with the *tetrarch* at the point, and senior troopers riding in the middle and at each end of the 13-man base line. The *ilarch* was probably accompanied by a trumpeter to relay signals to the four troop commanders, and a *hypēretes* to help him administer the squadron. The four wedges would be drawn up in a squadron battle line with sufficient intervals in between each troop to ensure that each had space to manoeuvre, and none collided with each other in the charge (which frequently happens, because the frontage of each troop expands in the charge as the galloping horses try to move away from each other).

It was the battle-aim of Alexander to advance his army obliquely so as to cause dislocations in the Persian line as they attempted to outflank him on his right. The Persian cavalry column attempting to turn his right flank would be kept at bay by successive charges of his light cavalry, delivered squadron by squadron. As the Persian cavalry was forced to move further to the right, they would eventually lose contact with their main battle line.

As soon as this dislocation was observed in the Persian battle line, Alexander personally led the decisive charge of his heavy cavalry straight for it. None of this was possible until new cavalry formations were developed in the early 4th century: cavalry formations which allowed the squadrons to redeploy rapidly and reorient the axis of attack. The wedge gave this flexibility to Alexander's cavalry, which is vividly illustrated in Curtius' description of the cavalry fighting at Issus which took place when a massive Persian cavalry column charged the Thessalian cavalry.

'But on the right the Persians were strongly attacking the Thessalian horsemen, and

Head of a cavalryman from the Alexander Mosaic in Pompeii. The silvering of the Boeotian helmet, the golden wreath, and the white horsehair plume are probably all insignia of senior officer rank. (German Archaeological Institute, Rome)

already one squadron had been ridden down by their very onset, when the Thessalians, smartly wheeling their horses about, slipped aside and returning to the fray, with great slaughter, overthrew the barbarians, whom confidence in their victory has scattered and thrown into disorder.'

A number of *ilai*, usually two, three or four, might be formed into a cavalry brigade, or *hipparchy*, commanded by a *hipparch*. At first the number of squadrons per brigade was variable, but later on the

Two plaques of a large sculpted relief discovered in 1948 and now in the National Museum, Athens. Dating from Alexander's time or shortly afterwards, it shows a cavalry officer's horse with pantherskin shabraque. The groom, a black African slave, wears a short tunic and boots. Traces of a Boeotian helmet painted at the back of the relief can still be made out.

system became more standardised.

Each cavalryman was allowed a groom, who may have been mounted, to look after his horse and equipment. The grooms were stationed behind the squadron in battle. The cavalrymen owned their own horses, though it was customary for a man drafted into the cavalry to be granted an initial 'establishment' to enable him to purchase a mount of suitable quality. Horses lost in action were replaced from the army pool of remounts. Alexander and the rest of the cavalry normally marched on foot to spare the horses, as troopers have done throughout history, and the horses were left unbridled unless action was imminent. The Greeks used a very severe bit with spiked 'hedgehog' rollers, which could ruin the horse's delicate mouth if left bridled too long.

Cavalry Equipment

Alexander, it seems, replaced the 'Phrygian' helmet, probably painted in regimental colours, with the Boeotian helmet left plain bronze. The cavalry helmets on the Alexander Sarcophagus and the Pompeiian mosaic seem to show insignia of rank, as was normal Greek practice. One helmet on the mosaic is silvered, with a gold wreath and a horsehair 'tail' fixed on the crown; one helmet on the sarcophagus is plain bronze with a white or silver wreath, and a second helmet on the mosaic is

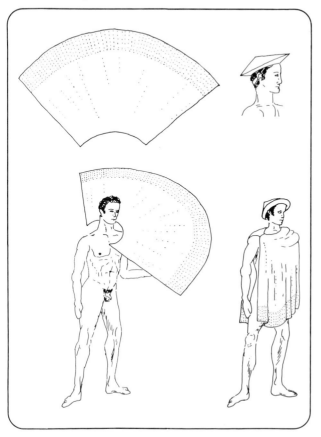

plain bronze with a white horsehair 'tail'. These could be the insignia of an *ilarch*, a *tetrarch* and a senior trooper respectively. It is known that Alexander gave gold crowns to his troops as an award for bravery, however, so this could be an alternative, though less likely, explanation for the wreaths (one of which is silver). The figure on the sarcophagus with a wreathed helmet also wears bracelets. These are certainly badges of rank, as gold bracelets and chains were used as insignia of rank by the Persians.

The long cavalry spear (*xyston*), though made of strong cornel wood, frequently shattered in action, so it was fitted with a second spearhead at the butt end to enable the trooper to continue fighting if this should happen. The *xyston* was not couched under the arm like a knight's lance, but was used to stab at the unprotected faces of the enemy horse and rider. The Persian cavalry, using a pair of shorter spears as javelins and fighting-spears, found themselves at a considerable disadvantage against *xysta*. The sword, a secondary weapon, was slung under the left arm, so it is frequently obscured by the cloak in surviving representations. We may guess that it was used principally as a stabbing weapon too, as the cavalry used straight swords in place of the curved sabres (*kopides*) we might have expected. The aristocratic troopers may have preferred to use their own highly decorated swords, with gold embellishment and bone or ivory hilts, similar to those shown on the Alexander mosaic or those recently excavated from Philip's tomb. Greek cavalry did not use shields at this time, though it was normal for generals to be accompanied by their personal shield-bearers to enable them to fight on foot if necessary. In one incident during the Balkan campaigns Alexander orders the Personal Companions and Bodyguards to take up their shields and gallop up a hill, and on reaching the top half of them dismount to fight on foot.

Some cavalrymen wear only a short-sleeved tunic, but most wear a long-sleeved outer tunic over the first. Only the heavy cavalry regiments (Companion, Thessalian, and Allied) were issued with the cuirass. During the early campaigns, either

The Macedonian cloak; in the form of a rolled-out truncated cone, its two inner corners were pinned together. It can be recognised when worn by the single corner hanging both in front of and behind the figure, and by the straight bottom edge. Headdress would be either the beret-like Macedonian *kausia* **or a smaller version of the Thessalian sun-hat.**

because of the heat or from bravado, Alexander rarely wore a cuirass and this idiosyncracy may have been widely aped by the young noblemen in the heavy cavalry regiments, especially in the Companion Cavalry. Cavalry boots seem to have been standard throughout the cavalry; their pattern is clearly shown on bronzes of Alexander. A soft leather lining 'sock' is held in place by a strap-work over-boot with a sole and heel.

Looking at Plate C1 one could guess that the Greek saddle cloth, made of some shaggy felt-like substance, was dyed in the regimental colour and faced in the squadron colour. Thus it might be medium purple for the Companions, dark purple for the Thessalians, and rose for the *Prodromoi*, faced in green, red, yellow or some other squadron colour—but this is speculative. Over the saddle cloth a pantherskin shabraque is sometimes worn; perhaps they were restricted to officers. The shabraque is formed from the whole animal's pelt—paws, tail, mask and all. The pelt is slit down the spine from the back of the mask to the middle to enable it to be fitted over the horse's head. The neck hole is lined with material, again possibly in the squadron colour. Identical pantherskin shabraques are also shown in contemporary reliefs from Athens and Serrai in Macedonia. Persian saddle cloths are sometimes used. These probably do not represent booty, as highly decorated Persian saddle cloths were much favoured by the aristocracy and had long been a luxury import into the Greek world. The cuirass-girdle may also have been in the squadron colour.

Companion Cavalry

The Companion (*hetairoi*) Cavalry, the senior regiment of the army, was recruited from the noble youth of Macedonia. Diodorus gives the regiment's strength at the start of the expedition as 1,800, but perhaps some squadrons were left in Macedonia. The regiment was divided into eight squadrons, the first being the Royal Squadron (*basilikē ilē*), which was the vanguard (*agēma*) squadron of the regiment and held the position of honour in the battle line. The Royal Squadron, in whose ranks the Personal Companions fought, was maintained at double strength. The other seven squadrons, at the normal strength of 200 lances each, formed up on the left of the Royal Squadron according to the order of

This small marble head, broken from a battle relief, probably represents Alexander. The neck is tilted slightly to the left, the eyes uplifted and the mouth slightly open—all personal idiosyncracies of Alexander which were so well known as to be copied by his successors, in much the same way as Napoleon's contemporaries aped his habit of putting one hand inside his coat. (Metropolitan Museum of Art, New York)

precedence for the day. The line squadrons are generally named after their commanders in the texts, but each was recruited from a different area of Macedonia and their official designations were probably territorial. In Asia we hear of the squadrons of Bottiaea, Amphipolis, Apollonia, Anthemus, and the so-called 'Leugaean' squadron, and an Upper Macedonian squadron is mentioned during the Balkan Campaigns. The other squadron names are lost.

Two horsemen on the Alexander Sarcophagus can be identified as Companion Cavalrymen. They both wear long-sleeved tunics of medium purple and golden-yellow cloaks with medium purple borders. The cloak (*chlamys*) is of the Macedonian type, so they must be Macedonians, and the colours suggest an élite unit. Furthermore Diodorus (17.77.5) tells us that following the death of Darius Alexander distributed Persian cloaks with purple borders to the Companions. The same colour combination reappears in Hellenistic representations which may also be of Companions (see

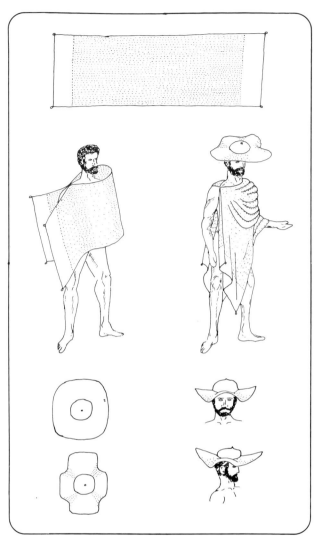

The Thessalian cloak; oblong in shape, it was pinned together along the top edge some distance from the corners, which were allowed to fall. It can be recognised by the two corners falling both in front of and behind the figure, and from its very uneven edge. Headdress would be the wide-brimmed Thessalian sun-hat.

The cuirass was made of small metal plates, linked together, lined or covered with leather or linen, in this case white, which made the cuirass resilient but at the same time more flexible. The length of Alexander's *xyston* has probably been exaggerated on the mosaic to fit the figures into the composition better.

Thessalian Cavalry

Our sources frequently state that the Thessalians were the best cavalry unit in the whole army. This is not surprising as they were raised from the aristocracy of Thessaly, the finest horsemen in the Greek world. For political and social reasons, however, the Companions were the senior regiment in the army and fought under Alexander's direct command, and the Thessalians were usually relegated to a position of lesser importance on the left wing.

Diodorus gives the Thessalians a strength of 1,800 on the crossing into Asia. This figure is the same as that given for the Companion Cavalry, and we may assume that the Thessalian regiment was organised in the same way too, that is divided into eight *ilai*. Their vanguard squadron was the Pharsalian *ilē*, the 'finest and most numerous' squadron (Arrian 3.11.10), which formed Parmenio's personal body-guard on the left wing at Gaugamela. It was the Thessalian regiment's counterpart to the Royal squadron of the Companions, and we may assume that it too was a double-strength squadron of 400. The names of the other seven *ilai* are not given by the historians, but it is fairly certain that they would have been named after the other principal cities of Thessaly in which they had been raised (such as Larisa, Pherae, Tricca, Pharcadon, Pelinna, Oloo-son and Philippi/Philippopolis—ancient Gomphi). Two hundred Thessalian horse joined the army at Gordium, but these were probably used to make up losses in the existing squadrons, rather than to create a ninth *ilē*.

The Thessalian regiment was disbanded at Ecbatana, when the allied contingents were sent back to Greece, but 130 volunteers stayed with the army. These Thessalian volunteers were formed into their own small unit, 'but even this little squadron soon wearied of endless hardship in the pursuit of Bessus, and after less than a year of mercenary service under the former hipparch

Head, p. 104).

On the Pompeiian mosaic Alexander appears wearing the uniform of an officer of Companion Cavalry. He is shown bare-headed for artistic reasons, but a small marble head broken from a battle-relief shows him wearing the standard Boeotian helmet of the cavalry. He also wears a purple cloak with golden-yellow border, the badge of a Personal Companion or Friend, in place of the standard regimental colours. We may presume, by comparison with Plate C2, that the rest of the regiment also normally wore a white cuirass of similar type with a girdle in the squadron colour.

Another Roman gold medallion from Tarsus shows Alexander out hunting. A short hunting spear has replaced the *xyston*, but otherwise the details of Alexander's dress and equipment concur with our other evidence. Note the pantherskin shabraque. The curve of the lower edge of the cuirass over the abdomen is probably an anachronism. (Bibliothèque Nationale, Paris)

Philippus, it was finally disbanded before the Oxus was crossed.' (H. D. Westlake, *Thessaly in the Fourth Century* BC, p. 227–8).

Two horsemen on the Alexander Sarcophagus, one at the hunt and one in battle, wear the distinctive Thessalian cloak—the national dress of Thessaly, identifiable by the two points hanging down both in front and behind the figure. These cloak-ends used to billow out behind the galloping horseman and gave the cloak its Greek nickname of 'Thessalian wings'. The two horsemen are certainly members of the Thessalian cavalry. These cloaks are a very dark purple in colour, with a white border at each end. Both men wear a short-sleeved red under-tunic, but only the fighting Thessalian wears a purple long-sleeved tunic on top. Otherwise the details of dress are similar to the Companions, or general for the whole cavalry; the white cuirass, similar to that worn by Alexander on the Issus mosaic, should be noted.

The Allied Horse

The Greek states of the Corinthian League were obliged to make contributions both of cavalry and of infantry to the expeditionary force. Clearly, not all these states were asked to furnish cavalry.

Diodorus tells us that 600 Greek horse under the command of Erigyius crossed to Asia with the army. These are probably the three squadrons mentioned as fighting under Erigyius at Gaugamela; the squadron of Peloponnesian and Achaean horse, the cavalry of Phthiotis and Malis, and the squadron of Locrian and Phocian horse. At the Granicus the allied cavalry were commanded by Philip son of Menelaus; this is presumably a temporary command, but we are not told why Erigyius was absent from the battle. Reinforcements which reached the army at Gordium included a further 150 horsemen from Elis. 'The Peloponnesian and other allied cavalry' fight with Parmenio on the left wing at Issus, but their commander is not given.

No Greek city seems to have made an individual contribution of a full squadron; rather, each squadron seems to be formed by brigading together the various contingents from a particular area. Our sources do not give us a complete picture of all the reinforcements reaching the army in Asia; information concerning the expansion of the army before the Gaugamela campaign is particularly lacking. We know that Alexander did not take all the army into Egypt, but left a portion of it in Syria. Whilst the ancient authors dwell at length on Alexander's activities in Egypt and mention the reinforcements reaching him there, we know virtually nothing about what had been happening to the rest of the army. The allied cavalry had been detached to the satrap of Syria after the battle of Issus, and it probably received further reinforcements while stationed there. Even before Issus, Curtius reports a speech delivered to Darius by the Greek soldier of fortune Charidemus which mentions 'the Thessalian horse and the Acarnanians and Aetolians', so it is possible that an Acarnanian and Aetolian squadron had already reached the army; but this speech may just be rhetoric invented by Curtius and put into the mouth of Charidemus to enliven his account. We are certain, though, that a Boeotian squadron reached the army in Asia, for an inscription found at Orchomenus records a dedication made by men who had served with Alexander in Asia and mentions their *ilarch*.

At Gaugamela, then, we hear of one brigade of Allied Horse (*hoi xymmachoi hippeis*) commanded by Erigyius son of Larichus, consisting of the squadron

The bronze Boeotian helmets worn by the cavalry were made by hammering out sheet bronze on an armourer's workshop model. This interesting example of such a model, carved from limestone, was found in Memphis; it is possibly of a later date. (Allard Pierson Museum, Amsterdam)

of Peloponnesians and Achaeans, the squadron of Phthiotis and Malis, and the squadron of Locris and Phocis. I presume these are the 600 who crossed into Asia with Erigyius. On the opposite (left) wing, however, we hear of a second brigade of Allied Horse commanded by Coeranus. I would guess that the second brigade also numbered 600 and was divided into three squadrons, probably including a squadron of Boeotians, and possibly including a squadron of Acarnanians and Aetolians. The Eleians could have either fought in the Peloponnesian and Achaean squadron on the right or in a third squadron on the left. The regiment of Allied Horse was disbanded at Ecbatana, but many men enrolled into the Mercenary Horse.

From their position in the various battles we can probably assume that the Allied Horse were a unit of heavy cavalry. Unfortunately no details of their dress or equipment have survived (but see Plates E2, E3).

The Prodromoi

Prodromoi or 'scouts' is a name usually applied only to the four squadrons of Thracian light cavalry belonging to the Royal Army, but occasionally to the other squadrons of Thracian auxiliary cavalry serving with the army too. The *prodromoi* of the Royal Army were probably recruited from inside the borders of Macedonia, from the Thracian provinces annexed by Philip, and served under Macedonian officers. The light cavalry squadrons seem to have been somewhat under strength at the crossing of the Hellespont, for Diodorus tells us that the *prodromoi* and the Paeonian squadron only numbered 900. Presumably the *prodromoi*, the Paeonian squadron and the Odrysian cavalry were brought fully up to strength by the reinforcement of 500 Thracian cavalry which reached the army at Memphis. A further reinforcement of 600 joined the army in Sittacene.

The Thracian cavalry were a wild, uncivilised group of soldiery, who would compare well to the Croats of the Thirty Years' War. They were much given to drink, women and booty. These habits seem to have been adopted by the Macedonian officers set over them. When King Alexander gave over the city of Thebes for plunder, one Alexander, the Macedonian commander of an *ilē* of Thracians but 'in no way like his namesake', broke into the house of a noblewoman called Timocleia. 'Without showing the least respect for the ancestry or the estate of the woman' he drank the cellar dry, had his pleasure of Timocleia, and then forced her to show him where the family gold was hidden. She told him it was hidden at the bottom of a well in the garden; and the avaricious *ilarch* would not wait till morning to inspect the loot, but climbed down the well immediately, dressed only in his tunic. Timocleia promptly repaid his bad manners by rolling boulders down the well and burying him alive. On hearing of the incident the king spared Timocleia and her family on account of her bravery.

The primary role of the *prodromoi*, as the name indicates, was to scout ahead of the advancing army. For this purpose they were occasionally brigaded with units of light infantry or detachments of heavy cavalry. During the Balkan campaigns some units of cavalry used javelins; these are probably *prodromoi*, who seem to have been equipped with the *xyston* and javelins in the first years of Alexander's reign. After the crossing of the Hellespont, however, the terms *prodromoi* and *sarissophoroi* are used indiscriminately and javelins are never mentioned again, so it seems that Alexander re-equipped them with the infantry pike before the expedition crossed over.

As far as defensive armament is concerned, we know from scattered references that the *prodromoi* did use helmets, but probably no other body-armour. A wall-painting in a chamber tomb, known as the 'Kinch' tomb from the name of its Danish excavator, provides us with some uniform details for the light cavalry. The tomb was discovered near Naoussa in Central Macedonia, some distance from the Thracian provinces in which the *prodromoi* were recruited. This is no obstacle to our identification, however, as the unit was commanded by senior officers drawn from the Macedonian nobility. The horseman is shown bearded, so the relief must date to Philip's reign, not Alexander's; he is spearing a Persian infantryman with his *xyston*. It is logical to assume that the horseman died fighting as a member of the advanced force Philip sent into Asia in the spring of 336. Duncan Head (p. 105) has also identified the painting with the *prodromoi*. Upon Alexander's accession or shortly afterwards the beards would be shaved off, bronze Boeotian helmets would be substituted for the painted 'Phrygian' helmets, and *sarissai* for *xysta*. The horse has the ubiquitous pantherskin shabraque, but it does not seem to be lined in any squadron colour. The regimental colour would seem to be the rose colour of the cloak and the trunk of the tunic, but it is not possible to guess which of the other colours might have been a squadron colour.

Thracian Cavalry

The four squadrons of the Royal Army were supplemented by further squadrons of auxiliary Thracian cavalry. The Paeonian squadron crossed the Hellespont with the army. The Paeonians seem to be a detachment of cavalry contributed to the expedition by the client king of Paeonia, for they are commanded by a prince of the Paeonian royal house called Ariston. The Odrysian cavalry were probably contributed in a similar way by the king of the Odrysians, but they were under the command of a Macedonian, Agathon son of Tyrimmas. The Odrysians joined the expedition in time to take part in the battle of Granicus. They were probably two squadrons strong at Gaugamela.

While we may assume that the Paeonian and Odrysian squadrons were equipped in a similar fashion to the regular squadrons of *prodromoi*, their general appearance and dress could have been markedly different as they were not part of the Royal Army. A Paeonian coin shows a warrior,

This bronze Boeotian helmet was found in June 1854 in the bed of the Tigris River at the confluence with its tributary the Sert (the ancient 'Centrites') near Tille in present-day Turkey. Mr R. B. Oakley of Oswaldkirk, Yorkshire, was travelling down the Tigris to Mosul by raft. One of the boatmen pushed his boathook into the stream to keep the raft from running ashore, and when he lifted it out of the water this helmet was caught on the hook! It was bought for the equivalent of about one shilling, and brought to Britain; at one time donated to Rugby School, it is now in the Ashmolean Museum, Oxford. (Ashmolean Museum)

dressed in a long-sleeved tunic, wearing a crested 'Attic' helmet, and equipped with a spear, riding a horse with a pantherskin saddle cloth. He spears a warrior on foot who is shown wearing trousers. Coins of this series have been identified with an incident in the Gaugamela campaign when Ariston, the commander of the Paeonian squadron, speared Satropates through the throat. The identification, however, is still far from certain.

Alexander was in process of crossing the Tigris; the infantry were wading across with considerable difficulty, but the king, together with a small advance party of light cavalry, had reached the far bank. Suddenly a flying column of 1,000 Persian cavalry commanded by Satropates appeared to dispute the crossing. The situation was critical— only the advance party was formed up on the river bank and the unformed infantry, struggling in the water with their packs, would fall easy prey to a quick charge. Alexander immediately ordered forward the Paeonian squadron, with Ariston at its head. From the river the whole army watched the drama unfolding on the steep riverbank.

Ariston made straight for the Persian colonel, Satropates, and promptly ran him through the throat with his spear. The Persian turned and tried to make his way back to safety among his comrades.

A broken relief in Bursa Museum, Turkey, found recently in the vicinity of that town. The lower part of this interesting sculpture shows heavy cavalry attacking Greek(?) infantry. Note the Boeotian helmets, the cuirasses, and the Greek and Persian saddle cloths. The piece must date to the reign of Alexander or shortly thereafter. (German Archaeological Institute, Istanbul)

Ariston overtook his victim, unhorsed him, and, after a brief but desperate struggle, severed his head with a sword-cut. The Paeonian prince gathered up Satropates' head and galloped back to the King, to the accompaniment of wild cheering from the army. Throwing his trophy at Alexander's feet the Paeonian shouted, 'Among us, oh King, such a present is rewarded with a golden drinking-horn!' 'An empty one, I suppose,' replied Alexander with a laugh, 'but I promise you one full of untempered wine.'

The Mercenary Cavalry

Alexander was deficient in light cavalry in his early campaigns. The mercenary cavalry were raised to offset this deficiency, a serious one, particularly in the Gaugamela campaign, where Alexander's strategic planning relied heavily on precise information as to the whereabouts of the enemy. We hear of a squadron of 200 mercenary cavalry as early as the siege of Halicarnassus, but these troops were left in Caria as part of the provincial army.

At Gaugamela we hear of two brigades of mercenary horse, the 'Foreign Mercenary Cavalry' under Andromachus son of Hieron and the 'Mercenary Cavalry' under Menidas. It is usually assumed that the latter unit is to be identified with the 400 Greek mercenaries who joined the expedition at Memphis under the command of 'Menoitas son of Hegesander'. The 'Foreign Mercenary Cavalry' were presumably of the same strength, two squadrons, but we are not told whether they had been raised earlier or at the same time as Menidas' unit, possibly in Syria.

Alexander seems to have considered these new, and as yet untried regiments to have been expendable. At Gaugamela Andromachus' unit is stationed in front of the left wing, while Menidas rides point to the whole army on the right wing. Battle commenced when Alexander ordered Menidas to charge the Scythian and Bactrian brigades of armoured cavalry, the latter unit alone some thousand sabres strong. The mercenary cavalry certainly earned their pay on 30 September 331 BC, and Menidas himself all but died of multiple arrow wounds received later on in the battle.

When the Greek allies were dismissed at Ecbatana, Alexander encouraged all who wished to continue to serve in the army to enrol as mercenaries, and we are told that many did so. The mercenary cavalry was expanded with those of the Allied Horse who signed on, supplemented with newly recruited mercenaries sent east, and the new units were commanded by officers previously serving in the Allied Horse. The precise details are obscure, and the evidence is open to various interpretations, but the picture *seems* to be as follows.

Both Menidas and Andromachus together with their troops were left behind under Parmenio in Media when Alexander pushed on to hunt down Darius. Soon after we hear that command of the 'Mercenary Cavalry' had passed to Philip son of Menelaus, who had commanded the Allied Horse at the Granicus. Andromachus retained command of the 'Foreign Mercenary Cavalry'. Meanwhile we hear that Alexander has taken the Mercenary Cavalry under Erigyius with him. In the middle of 330, therefore, there are at least three units of mercenary horse.

One year later, during operations near Samarkand, Alexander hears that the garrison left behind in that city was being besieged by Spitamenes. He sends back a relief column consisting of about 60 Companions, 800 mercenary horse, and a detachment of mercenary infantry, retaining one *hipparchy* of mercenary horse under his command. The whole of the relief column, worn out by a long forced march, was ambushed by Scythian horse-archers and exterminated while trying to withdraw towards the River Polytimetus. Only 40 cavalry and about 300 infantry escaped.

The relief column was rather ineffectually commanded by Pharnuches, and under him are mentioned Menedemus, who presumably commanded the infantry, as well as Andromachus and Caranus, each, presumably, commanding 400 cavalry. During the account of the fighting Caranus, who may possibly be identified with the Coeranus who commanded the second brigade of Allied Horse at Gaugamela, is called a *hipparch*, but there is no indication anywhere that he holds any authority over Andromachus. It seems wisest to conclude that there continued to be three units of mercenary horse, each two *ilai* strong, each now called a *hipparchy*. Caranus may have taken over command of one of these units from Erigyius or Philip, but it is just possible that there were four hipparchies, the fourth having escaped from our texts.

The description of the unequal fight between Menidas' cavalry and the Bactrians at Gaugamela makes it obvious that the mercenary horse were but lightly equipped. Probably they fought with spear and swords and wore only the Boeotian helmet, boots, tunic and cloak. No representation survives which can be associated with the regiment, but their appearance was probably identical to that of the *prodromoi*, only the colours being different.

The Infantry

Organisation and Tactics

At the lowest level the tactical unit of the infantry was the *dekas* which, as the name implies, had once consisted of ten men, expanded to 16 well before Alexander's reign. The *dekas* formed one file of the phalanx.

Normally the files would be drawn up in close order (*pyknos, pyknōsis*), 16 deep with each man occupying a yard square. Locked shields (*synaspismos*) was a formation usually only adopted when receiving rather than delivering a charge. It was achieved by inserting the rear half of each file into the spaces between the front halves of the file. The depth of the phalanx would now be eight yards, with each man occupying a frontage of one cubit (half a yard). Both formations, however, were found to be too cramped for manoeuvring or advancing in an orderly manner, so prior to contact the phalanx would be drawn up in an open order with a depth of two files (32 yards) with each double file occupying a frontage of two yards. This was probably called 'deep order' (*bathos*) in Alexander's army. In all these formations, obviously, the frontage occupied by the phalanx remained constant.

During all these evolutions the spear would not be lowered, as it would obstruct free manoeuvre; the lowering of the spears was only ordered before the charge, which was sometimes carried out at the run if rapid movement were required to exploit the tactical situation. The charge would be delivered to the accompaniment of the Macedonian battle-cry—'Alalalalai!'—offered to Enyalios, a Greek epithet for Ares, the god of war. The prior advance was, in contrast, carried out in perfect silence to give the battle-cry maximum psychological effect.

The army usually marched in column, it seems, with the phalanx split into two wings. The exact manner in which the phalanx would deploy from column into line is not, as yet, fully understood, but the advance of the phalanx in ever closer formation is nicely described in an account of the battle of Issus written by the contemporary historian Callisthenes (and contained in Polybius 12.19.6):

> 'Immediately on issuing into the open country he re-formed his order, passing to all the word of command to form into phalanx, making it at first 32 deep, changing this subsequently to 16 deep, and finally as he approached the enemy to 8 deep.'

Alexander, at the end of his life, intended to incorporate Persian archers and javelinmen into the phalanx, and Arrian's account of the proposed change (7.23.3–4) mentions that the file was commanded by a *dekadarch*, and contained a *dimoirites* and two *dekastateroi* or 'ten-stater men'.

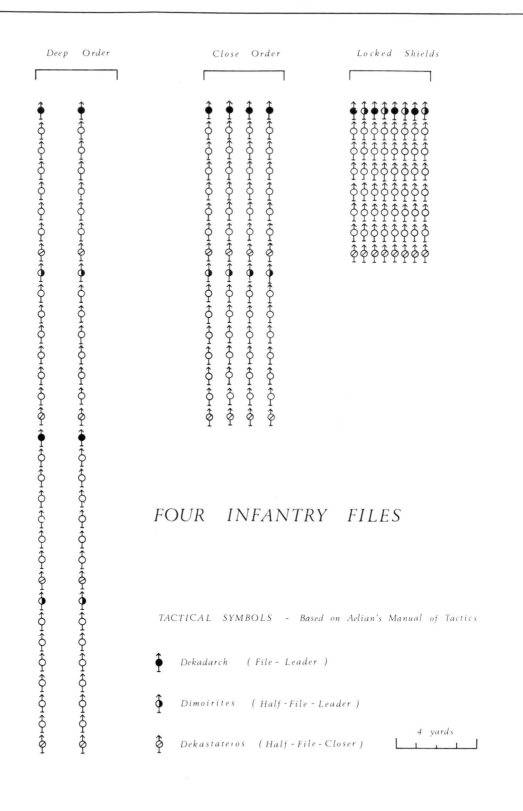

Deep Order   Close Order   Locked Shields

FOUR INFANTRY FILES

TACTICAL SYMBOLS - Based on Aelian's Manual of Tactics

Dekadarch   *(File - Leader)*

Dimoirites   *(Half - File - Leader)*

Dekastateros   *(Half - File - Closer)*

4 yards

1: Alexander, as senior officer of Companion Cavalry
2: Companion cavalryman

A

1: Companion cavalryman, hunting dress
2: Royal Page, hunting dress
3: Personal Companion, hunting dress

B

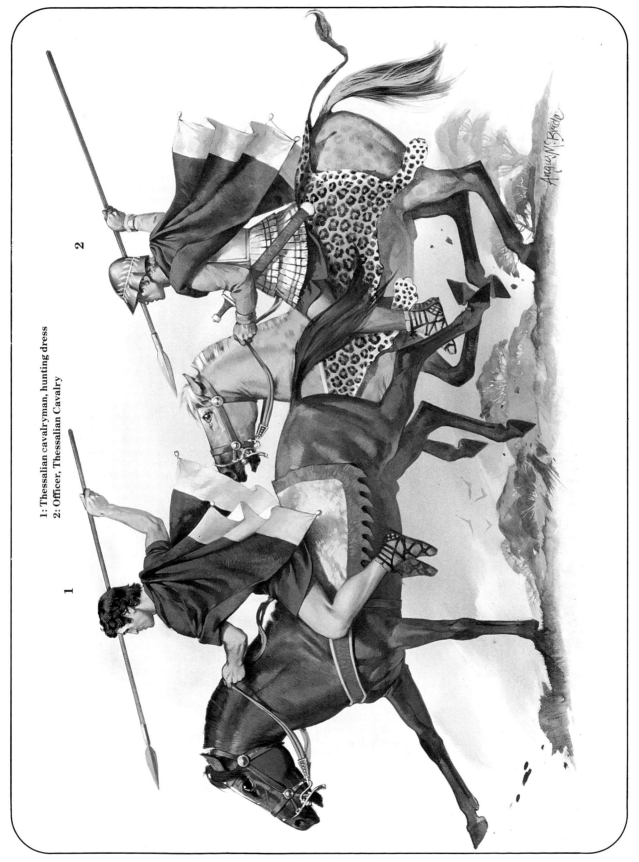

1: Thessalian cavalryman, hunting dress
2: Officer, Thessalian Cavalry

C

1: Cavalryman of the 'Prodromoi'
2: Infantryman, camp dress
3: Foot Companion, hunting dress

D

1: Hypaspist
2, 3 : Soldiers of unidentified unit

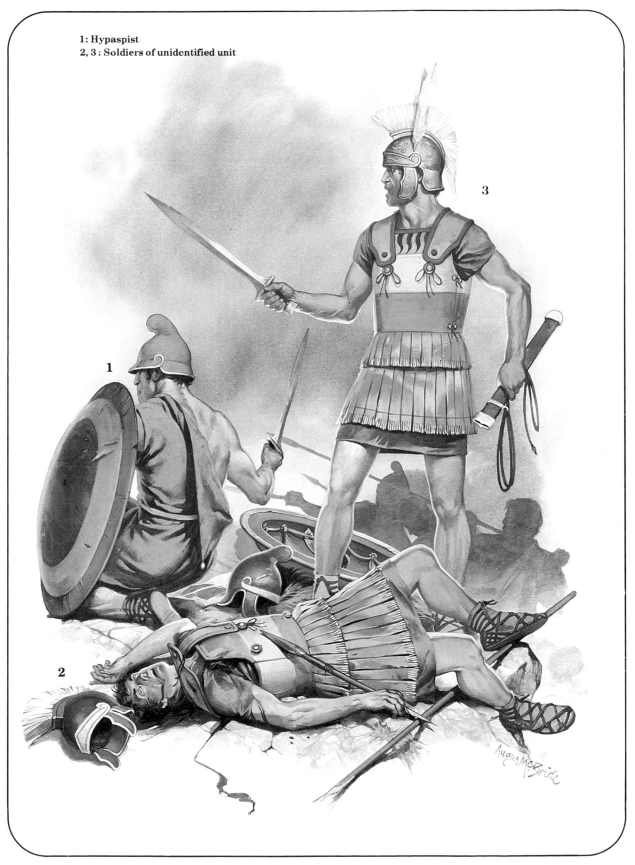

E

1: Foot Companion
2: Greek mercenary in Persian service
3: Officer of Foot Companions

F

1: Senior soldier of Foot Companions
2: Foot Companion
3: Servant

G

1: Javelinman
2: Senior rank of an unidentified unit
3: Allied Greek infantryman

H

Coin of King Antimachos II of Bactria. Only fragments remain of the history of the Greeks and Macedonians in the East after the time of Alexander; we know that they conquered the Punjab, and many embraced Buddhism. They were eventually overrun by steppe tribes from the north. Antimachos is shown wearing the beret-like *kausia*, national headdress of Macedonia, and the royal diadem; Alexander is mentioned as wearing the same combination on occasion.

Dimoirites literally means something like 'two-part man' and is usually translated as 'double-pay man', which is its sense in Xenophon. In Hellenistic times, however, the 16-man file was divided into four quarters, and the half-file is called a *dimoiria* and is commanded by a *dimoirites* (Asclepiodotus 2.2), so this is probably a better interpretation. Originally, then, it seems that the *dekadarch* commanded the file and the first half-file, and the *dimoirites*, standing in the ninth rank of the file, led the second half-file. The two *dekastateroi* probably brought up the rear of each half-file and stood in the eighth and 16th ranks. These senior soldiers were the equivalent of our junior NCOs.

An infantry company (*lochos*) would consist of 512 men drawn up in 32 files and so would occupy a frontage of 32 yards. It was the basic administrative and organisational unit of the infantry and we hear of no sub-divisions. The *lochos* was commanded by an officer called a *lochagos*. Later on in Alexander's reign the company is sometimes called a 'five-hundred' and its commander a *pentekosiarch* or 'commander of five-hundred'. We may also assume that each company also had a *hyperetes* and a trumpeter to pass on orders. A number of companies, usually two or three, would comprise a battalion or *taxis*. In some regiments the battalion was called a 'thousand' or *chiliarchy*, but this term was never used if the battalion had more than two *lochoi*.

On the march

Each *dekas* was allowed one servant to look after its heavy baggage, which was carried by a baggage animal, usually a mule or donkey. When the army reached Egypt, and afterwards, an increasing use was made of camels, who were able to carry more and who were more suitable for campaigning in Asia. The servants were called *ektaktoi*, or supernumeraries, because they did not fight in the ranks.

The bulkiest items the *dekas* had were its tents. We do not know how many men constituted a tent-party, whether a full file, half-file, or quarter-file. The tents were carried in waterproof leather tent-covers which acted as fly-sheets when the tents were erected. During river crossings these tent-covers were sewn together and stuffed with chaff to make floating rafts. Usually the animals would be ferried across on these rafts while the men would cross over supported by inflated water-skins. The water-skins would normally be carried by the baggage animal, as would the iron tent pegs and the guy ropes. We hear of axes being used, and we know that each *dekas* carried a hand-mill: presumably other implements and construction tools were issued down to the level of the *dekas*.

The infantry usually marched with their own weapons and armour, but the uncomfortable helmet was replaced by the *kausia*, a beret-style cap, the regional headdress of Macedonia. A personal pack was also carried. We know this included a bed-roll, for in India the men had to sleep with their bedding slung from the trees to get away from the snakes. It would also include a drinking cup and other domestic items. The men also carried their own food, which would be ready-cooked if rapid movement were required. Cooking was extremely slow and difficult in the days before flint and steel came into use during the Middle Ages. It was normal Greek military practice to carry fire in some form or other inside earthenware pots.

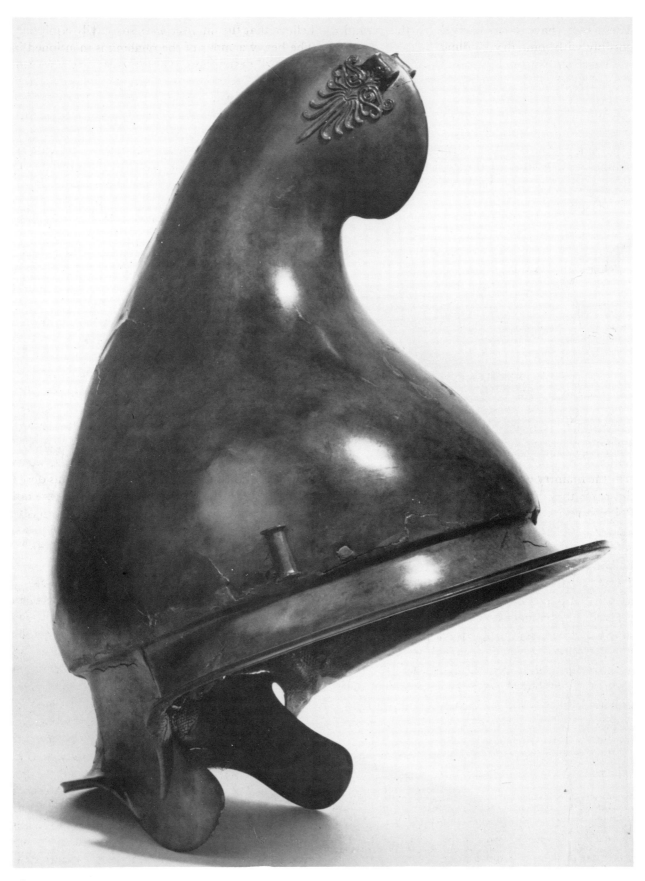

These may have been carried by the servants, possibly with some dry kindling.

The other personal possessions of the soldiery were carried in the baggage wagons, as was their booty. The sick also travelled in wagons, possibly in special ambulances. The baggage train consisted of these wagons and others containing artillery and siege engines in kit form, accompanied by the families of the soldiers and the sutlers following the army, marching at the back of the army protected by a rearguard.

An interesting passage in Curtius (6.2.16) describes the scene in camp when the army is gripped by a rumour that the king is about to return to Macedonia:

> 'They ran as though crazed to their tents and made ready their packs for the journey; you would believe that the signal to march had been given throughout the whole camp. Here the noise of those looking for their tent-mates, there of those loading the wagons, was borne to the king's ears.'

Infantry Equipment

The infantrymen on the Alexander Sarcophagus all use hoplite shields. Most modern authorities believe that the infantry under Alexander continued to use the *peltai* they had used during the first years of Philip's reign, but this view runs against the archaeological evidence, and against some evidence contained in the texts. In one battle during the Balkan campaigns Arrian (1.1.9) tells us that the Thracians intended to launch carts down a hillside to break up the advancing phalanx. Alexander ordered the phalanx to crouch down and link their shields closely together. The carts slid over the shields and not one man perished. It is difficult to see how this operation could have been successfully performed without large shields. Curtius mentions similar 'tortoise' tactics being used during the campaign against the Uxians and the storming of the Persian Gates.

Many infantrymen on the Sarcophagus also wear cuirasses, but again most modern authorities do not

An interesting helmet of the 'Phrygian' type, recently excavated and published by Mrs J. Votokopolou, the Ephor of Ioannina Museum, who has kindly supplied the photograph. Though possibly a little later than Alexander's reign, it is useful in that the tubular plume-holders fixed to the visor give us some idea of how to reconstruct the plumes attached to the helmets of Alexander's infantry.

believe that the infantry were so heavily equipped. The heavy armour of the phalanx is mentioned in Arrian's description (1.28.7) of the Pisidian campaign, however, and Diodorus (17.44.2) tells us that the Tyrians poured hot sand over their Macedonian besiegers, which passed underneath cuirasses and clothing and brought about a horrible death. Finally Diodorus (17.95.4) mentions that 25,000 infantry panoplies were issued in India, and Curtius (9.3.22) adds that the old sets were burned. It seems, then, that at least some of the infantry used cuirasses, manufactured in part from some combustible material such as linen or leather.

The helmets are of the 'Phrygian' type: some helmets are left plain bronze, but most are painted blue, which may have been the distinguishing colour of the infantry. A few helmets have gilt spines running along the 'cockscomb' crest, and this may be an officer's badge of rank. These and other helmets without the spine have fittings for plumes, which are missing from the Sarcophagus. The plumes have been restored as long feathers, from one helmet painted behind a figure on the Sarcophagus, and from coins showing Alexander. One helmet in a later Macedonian wall-painting shows plumes in the form of horsehair 'tails', however, and restorations incorporating this detail are equally possible. Swords and scabbards are not shown on some of the figures, but it would seem that the artist had deliberately chosen to leave them out, and we can probably assume that all the infantry were issued with swords.

No spears are shown in use on the Sarcophagus. The infantry used a long spear of Balkan origin called the *sarissa*. Theophrastus in his *Historia Plantarum* (3.12.1–2) tells us that the longest [*sic*] *sarissai* measured 12 cubits (18 feet), but he compiled this work after becoming professor at Athens in 322 BC, so this only gives us a maximum length for the spears used by the armies of Alexander's successors. *Sarissai* may have been shorter during Alexander's reign, but even so one presumes that they would have been held underarm with both hands.

Apart from its length the most distinctive feature of the *sarissa* was its small iron head, which made it more suitable for piercing armour than the large-headed Greek hoplite spear. A Roman writer on hunting (Grattius, *Cynegeticon* 117–120) warns us to

avoid the enormous Macedonian pikes with their small 'teeth' as unsuitable for hunting. The *sarissa* seems to have been furnished with a spear-butt, although this is not absolutely certain. A bronze spear-butt in the Greek Museum of the University of Newcastle upon Tyne may provide us with such an example. This object has many interesting features and is well worth describing at some length (see accompanying photo). The spear-butt is cast and is very heavy; inside are traces of the pitch used to fix it to the shaft. During cleaning in 1977 black lettering was discovered at the top underneath the layers of corrosion. Between two narrow bands are the letters MAK, an abbreviation for 'Macedonian' and an indication that the piece was issued by the state. One is reminded of the 'WD broad arrow' used to this day to mark British Army property. Similar black-painted bands can be observed on some of the iron pike heads on the Pompeiian mosaic. A date in the later 4th century BC has been suggested for the spear-butt, but certainty is impossible.

The Foot Companions

The Foot Companions (*pezhetairoi*) numbered 9,000, divided into six battalions (*taxeis*) of three *lochoi* each. The *taxeis* were normally named after their commanders. Four *taxeis* had the same commanders down to 330 BC: those of Coenus son of Polemocrates, Perdiccas son of Orontes, Craterus son of Alexander, and Meleager son of Neoptolemus. The *taxis* of Amyntas son of Andromenes was temporarily commanded by his brother Simmias while Amyntas was back in Macedonia levying reinforcements. The last *taxis* was commanded by Philip son of Amyntas at Granicus, by Ptolemaios son of Seleucus at Issus, at which battle he was killed, and afterwards by Polyperchon son of Simmias. The battalions would be drawn up on the battlefield in order of precedence for the day, although Coenus' *taxis*, which seems to be of élite status, occupies the position of honour on the right wing at Issus and Gaugamela. Some of the *taxeis*, including Coenus', were termed *asthetairoi*, which could be a term for élite battalions or for battalions recruited in Upper Macedonia.

Bronze spear-butt: the lettering appeared during cleaning in 1977. (Greek Museum, University of Newcastle upon Tyne)

Detail of the Alexander Mosaic from Pompeii showing a stand of Macedonian pikes foreshadowing the doom of the Persian King Darius. Note the painted bands around the spear sockets. (German Archaeological Institute, Rome)

Each *taxis* was raised from a different district of Macedonia, from which it probably took its official designation. Unfortunately the 'ethnics' of the *taxeis* of the Foot Companions are only given in the descriptions of Alexander's forces at Gaugamela contained in Diodorus and Curtius, which, although based on a common source, differ from each other. Both are garbled and both differ from Arrian. The problem is still the subject of considerable scholarly debate, but one possible interpretation is that Coenus' *taxis* is Elymiotid, Perdiccas' is Orestid, Meleager's is Lyncestian, and Polyperchon's is Tymphiot. So it is possible that at least half of the six *taxeis* were recruited from the separatist cantons of Upper Macedonia; perhaps all were. This could be deliberate policy on Alexander's part, leaving only the more politically reliable battalions recruited from the heart of the kingdom back in Macedonia with Antipater.

Only five phalangites are shown clothed on the Alexander Sarcophagus, and of these four wear cuirasses. These figures certainly represent Foot Companions. No two figures are dressed and equipped alike, so one must assume that they represent four separate *taxeis*. No figure can be associated with a particular *taxis* with any certainty, but one of the four, clad in a purple tunic, may belong to an élite battalion—possibly *asthetairoi*, perhaps Coenus' Elymiotid battalion. The bronze shields have a coloured medallion painted in their centre. These seem to show the heads of deities, perhaps ones with local associations: probably each battalion had its own shield-device.

The Hypaspists

Hypaspistes means 'shield-bearer' in Greek. The official name of the regiment seems to have been 'The Hypaspists of the Companions' (*hoi hypaspistoi*

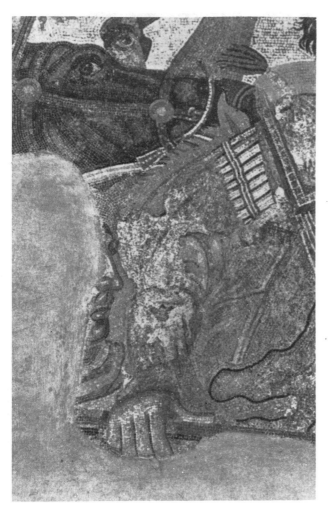

Detail of the Alexander Mosaic from Pompeii. This infantryman, wearing a purple *kausia* **and a red cloak, is possibly an officer of Hypaspists. (German Archaeological Institute, Rome)**

tōn hetairōn), and it is generally thought that the regiment had originally been formed from the personal retainers of the king's Companions. This role was continued in a vestigial manner, for the leading hypaspists carried the king's personal weapons, including the Sacred Shield of Troy, before him in battle. The regiment seems to have been 3,000 strong at first, divided into six *lochoi*, and was commanded by Nicanor son of Parmenio until his death in 330. We hear of a number of hypaspist officers in the texts: Admetus (possibly commander of the *agēma*), who dies at Tyre, Philotas, Hellanicus, Adaeus, who dies at Halicarnassus, and Timander. Adaeus is called a *chiliarch*, but this could be an anachronism.

The men of the vanguard *lochos* of the regiment

(*agēma*) were known as 'The Royal (*basilikoi*) Hypaspists', and were composed of men selected out of the whole army for their height. This *lochos* (possibly expanded to a *chiliarchy* later) guarded the king's tent in camp and always took the place of honour in the battle-line, the other companies forming up on the left in order of precedence for the day.

The Hypaspists acted as a flexible link between the Companion Cavalry and the Foot Companions. When the cavalry advanced the Hypaspists had to be able to move forward rapidly in order to keep up with them. It is logical to assume that they were more lightly equipped than the Foot Companions. In several places the texts talk of Alexander taking the lightest armed of the phalanx (or of the hoplites) with him, and we should assume that the Hypaspists are meant. Whenever Alexander detaches a 'flying column' from the army the Hypaspists always form part of it, as they would have been able to keep up with the pace much more easily than the heavily clad Foot Companions.

Of the five clothed hoplites on the Alexander Sarcophagus, one alone does not wear a cuirass, and we should identify this figure as a hypaspist. He is, in fact, wearing the dress and equipment of a Greek hoplite prior to Philip's re-armament. The tunic, let down at the shoulder to allow free movement of the right arm, was known as an *exōmis*. Alone of the infantry the hypaspist wears boots. During the long chases after Darius and Bessus the hypaspists are sometimes mounted two-a-back behind the cavalrymen on their horses, so perhaps boots were worn for such eventualities. In one of the descriptions of the murder of Cleitus, Arrian tells us that some sources say Alexander snatched a spear from a Bodyguard, others say it was a *sarissa* from one of the guards (presumably a hypaspist). A short broken spear is painted on the sarcophagus, together with a shield, lying next to the hypaspist. The spear may belong to him. Also lying next to him is a 'Phrygian' helmet, painted purple with a gilt spine, which could belong to an officer of hypaspists (see Plate E). Vestiges of the figure of a footsoldier, running alongside Alexander on the Pompeiian mosaic and wearing a purple *kausia* and a red (Macedonian?) cloak, may also show an officer of the hypaspists, as, we would expect this corps to be shown alongside the cavalry.

The Later Army

After Gaugamela the army took Babylon, then marched on Susa. On the road to Susa, passing through the fertile province of Sittacene, it was met by a large reinforcement from Macedonia under the command of Amyntas and consisting of 6,000 Macedonian foot, 600 Macedonian cavalry, 600 Thracian cavalry, 3,500 Trallians, and mercenaries to the number of 4,000 foot and 380 horse. Alexander halted the army and carried out the first of a series of thoroughgoing army re-organisations. He also took the opportunity to introduce some purely administrative reforms, and to promote officers of ability to the vacancies created.

The large number of reinforcements, even after replacing losses and releasing men from service, allowed Alexander to expand the infantry. Curtius seems to be talking of the hypaspists when he tells us that the *lochoi* were grouped into *chiliarchies* which had not existed before(?). New officers were appointed on the basis of military virtue; eight names follow (including Philotas and Hellanicus), so we may presume that the number of *lochoi* was raised to eight. It also seems that a seventh *taxis* was added to the Foot Companions. Next year Alexander leaves 6,000 Macedonian infantry (four *taxeis*) at Ecbatana to guard the treasure, but takes the Hypaspists and the *taxeis* of Coenus, Craterus and Amyntas with him in the pursuit of Darius and the Hyrcanian campaign. Seven *taxeis* are also mentioned at the Hydaspes.

The cavalry was also re-organised. Each *ilē* was now divided into two *lochoi* of two troops each, and officers were appointed to command on the basis of ability after a close scrutiny of the military conduct sheets. This reform was probably instituted to ease administrative efficiency, as the *ilē* was a rather large force of horses, grooms and riders for one man to administer effectively. Henceforward the cavalry was administered by century (*hekatostuas*), which word becomes interchangeable with *lochos* in the cavalry.

More major changes occurred when the army reached Ecbatana. The Thessalian cavalry and the Allied forces, both cavalry and infantry, were disbanded and sent home. Many, however, remained with the army as mercenaries, and in future much more use is made of mercenaries and Asian troops. Later in his reign Alexander starts to

The Azara herm, now in the Louvre. Found at Tivoli, it was presented to Napoleon by Don José Nicholas de Azara, international diplomat, patron of the arts, man of letters, archaeologist and antiquarian, and representative of the Spanish court first at Rome and later at Paris. The herm shows Alexander at the age of 30—increasingly superstitious, turbulent, and running out of geography. (Louvre, Paris)

levy and train Persian troops, and before his death he planned to integrate these troops into the phalanx.

During the early part of 330 BC, in preparation for the arduous campaigns lying ahead in the mountains and deserts of Iran and Central Asia, the Foot Companions start to lose their armour. A stratagem described in Polyaenus (4.3.13) tells us that Alexander re-equipped his soldiers with the half-cuirass (*hēmithōrakion*) instead of the cuirass, after they had fled, in order that they would not turn their backs on the enemy again. The incident referred to must be Alexander's first (and disastrous) attempt to storm the Persian Gates, and we should accept the information Polyaenus gives us as genuine, even if the reason given for the change is incorrect. During the Hyrcanian campaign Coenus' *taxis* is described as 'the lightest armed of the Macedonian phalanx'; 'the lightest armed of the

It was perhaps when the army entered India that the *sarissai* first reached their enormous length, giving the phalanx greater capability to fight elephants and their drivers. The cuirass had been discarded and normal equipment now consisted of shield, sword, javelin and *sarissa*, held in the left hand at first, then transferred to the right after the javelin had been thrown. At the Hydaspes sabres (*kopides*) are used to attack the trunks of Porus' elephants, and axes to cut off their feet.

The army in India must have presented a strange sight. Before the campaign Alexander had issued the Hypaspists with silvered shields, the cavalry with gilded bits, and the rest of the infantry with gilded and silvered equipment. This sumptuousness was mixed with shabbiness. The lines of supply had started to break down. At first Persian tunics had to be worn, then re-cut Indian ones; cuirasses and other armour wore out and had to be discarded. The morale of the troops had been severely undermined by Porus' elephants, and when a rumour hit the army that an army of 4,000 elephants lay ahead on the other side of the Hyphasis River they mutinied. This fear of elephants was probably the main consideration which induced Alexander to re-distribute armour to the infantry shortly afterwards: the main purpose of armour, after all, is not to protect the wearer, but to make him think he is protected.

Greek Infantry

Some 7,000 Greek allied infantry crossed the Hellespont with Alexander. The corps was composed of contingents sent by the member states of the League of Corinth; each contingent was composed of selected men (*epilektoi*) from the state's army, and served under its own officers. The corps as a whole was commanded by a Macedonian *strategos*.

Following the shattering blow delivered to them at Chaeronea, the armies of Greece underwent a series of army reforms aimed at upgrading their equipment so as to enable them to hold their own in the new conditions of general war. In Athens we can see the result of these reforms, carried out in that city under the aegis of the politician Lycurgus, in the gravestones sculpted between 338 and 317 (when ostentatious funerary monuments were banned). Body armour, abandoned since the

This Athenian sepulchral relief, found at Eleusis in 1888, shows the new equipment adopted by the Athenian army after the defeat at Chaeronea: bronze muscle-cuirass with leather groin-flaps, and bronze 'Phrygian' helmet after the Macedonian style. There are many representations of this type in the museums of Athens and Eleusis, all dating to the years 338–317 BC, and many still showing traces of the original colouring. All soldiers seem to wear a red tunic and *ephaptis* and some also wear head-bands. (National Museum, Athens)

phalanx' are mentioned a year later in operations near Maracanda; and in 326 in the advance to the Aornos Rock 'the lightest but at the same time the best [i.e. most suitably] armed' men are selected from *taxeis* other than that of Coenus. So it seems that other *taxeis*, or ranks of other *taxeis*, may have also started to use lighter equipment.

Peloponnesian Wars, is re-introduced in the form of the 'muscle-cuirass', and the Spartan-style *pilos* helmet is replaced by the Macedonian 'Phrygian' helmet. The situation recalls the late 19th century, when the world's armies threw away their shakos and képis and donned spiked helmets. In Megara we do not see the 'Phrygian' helmet appear, but a 'muscle-cuirass' of similar type to the Athenian was adopted. We can assume that similar changes took place in other states in Greece less well known archaeologically. One figure on the Alexander Sarcophagus (Plate H3) can be identified as a Greek, for he has not shaved his beard off, as he would have had to do had he been a member of the Macedonian Army. He also wears a 'muscle-cuirass'.

The army also contained a large number of Greek mercenary infantry. The main role of the mercenary infantry was to provide garrison troops

Originally in the Nani Collection in Venice, this stele was first published by Paciaudi in 1761. It was purchased by the Musée Calvet in 1841 among other marbles from the same collection. The inscription records the award of the office of *proxenos*—'state representative'—by the state of Athens to the Megarian general Phokinos, who wears the crested helmet of a general and who is followed by two other Megarians. All three wear the muscle-cuirass, but the 'Phrygian' helmet does not appear. (Musée Calvet, Avignon)

to keep newly conquered provinces in check. Troops for this purpose were frequently enrolled on the spot, usually from Greek mercenaries previously in Persian service. These mercenary bands were not altogether reliable; many had anti-Macedonian sympathies, and mutinies were not infrequent, particularly in the later years of Alexander's reign. Mercenaries were also used, however, to supplement the number of infantry in the field army, but these units seem to have been composed of altogether more reliable troops who had been with the army a long time or who had been recruited more recently from friendly states in Greece.

The surviving accounts of the battle of Gaugamela are all individually incomplete and differ significantly from one another, but they seem to mention two separate regiments of mercenaries participating in the battle. The veteran (*archaioi*) mercenaries, who fight on the right wing and are mentioned by Arrian, are probably the 5,000 who originally crossed the Hellespont with Alexander either in part or in full. The Achaean mercenaries, who fight on the left wing and are mentioned by Diodorus and Curtius (though Curtius does not call them Achaean), are probably the 4,000 mercenaries recruited in the Peloponnese which joined the army at Sidon the year before (Arrian 2.20.5).

Greek mercenary infantry at this time were still equipped along traditional Spartan lines, with bronze hoplite shield and helmet but no other body armour, carrying the normal infantry spear and sword, and dressed in red *exōmis* tunics. Certainly Greek mercenary infantry in Persian service appear with this dress and equipment on both the Alexander Sarcophagus (see Plate F2) and the Alexander Mosaic. It is possible that the mercenaries in Macedonian service wore cuirasses, but, given their position on the wings at Gaugamela, where mobility would be crucial, it is more probable that they did not.

Light Infantry

We know precious little of the light infantry (*psiloi*) of the army. They presumably fought in open order, perhaps in less depth than the phalanx, and their sub-units may have occupied greater frontages than those of the phalanx. The basic sub-unit seems to be the company of 500, but we are not sure if these companies were called *lochoi* as they were in the phalanx.

The corps of archers (*toxotai*) as a whole was under the command of a *stratēgos*, and was divided into a number of companies of 500 men, each, it seems, under the command of a *toxarch*. The first *stratēgos*, Cleander, died in the Pisidian campaign and was replaced by Antiochus, who in turn died and was replaced by the Cretan Ombrion in Egypt in 331 BC.

Alexander seems to have had a company of Cretan archers from the beginning of his reign. These Cretans could have been mercenaries, but it is more likely that they were an allied contingent supplied by those cities of Crete favourable to Macedon. They are not mentioned after the dismissal of the allies at Ecbatana. Cretan archers were equipped with a small bronze *peltē*, which

The tomb of Aristonautes, found in Athens in 1864, is well known and widely published. Aristonautes was an officer in the infantry; his dress and equipment are identical to those shown on other Attic tombstones of infantrymen of this period, but his helmet would originally have been circled by an applied metal wreath as the insignia of his rank—the peg-holes for the missing wreath are still visible in the helmet. (National Museum, Athens)

Bronze statuette of Alexander in the Museo Nazionale, Naples. (Anderson)

enabled them to fight at close quarters as well as provide missile fire. The Cretans served under their own officers—Eurybotas, who was killed at Thebes in 335, and thereafter by Ombrion, who was promoted to command of the whole corps of archers at Memphis in 331.

A second company of archers soon joined the expedition under the command of the *toxarch* Clearchus, who died during the siege of Halicarnassus. He seems to have been replaced by Antiochus, who is mentioned as a *toxarch* at Issus, although he doubled as *stratēgos* of the whole corps after the death of Cleander. We do not know the name of the *toxarch* appointed to command the second company after Antiochus' death in 331, nor do we know the nationality of the company, although they may have been Macedonians. A third company, under Briso, joins the expedition before Gaugamela, and these are definitely called Macedonians. The non-Cretans did not, it seems, carry the bronze *peltē*, for Arrian (3.18.5) refers to

'the lightest-armed of the archers' during the storming of the Persian Gates.

The Agrianian javelinmen, under the command of the Macedonian Attalus, were the crack light infantry unit of the army. Plate H1 shows a possible reconstruction of their dress, though *peltai* may have been carried as well as javelins. They were probably supplied for the expedition by the client king of the Agrianians, Langarus, out of his household troops. Only one company was present at the crossing of the Hellespont, but a second company joined the army before Issus, bringing up their strength to 1,000.

Little is known of the other light infantry, who are given the general term of 'Thracians' in the texts. They are the 7,000 Odrysians, Triballians and Illyrians who appear in Diodorus' enumeration of the army which crossed the Hellespont. They could be mercenaries, but given Alexander's shortage of money in the earlier campaigns they are more probably further contingents sent for the expedition by other client kings. Probably all the light infantry were javelinmen (*akontistai*), divided into a number of *taxeis*, although there may also have been some units of slingers. The whole corps may have been under the command of an obscure figure whom Arrian (4.7.2) calls 'Ptolemaios the *stratēgos* of the Thracians'. The Odrysians were

The Alexander Mosaic from Pompeii, a mosaic copy of a masterpiece by a Greek painter contemporary with Alexander. The author of the original work has not yet been identified with any certainty, but leading contenders are Apelles and Philoxenus. (German Archaeological Institute, Rome)

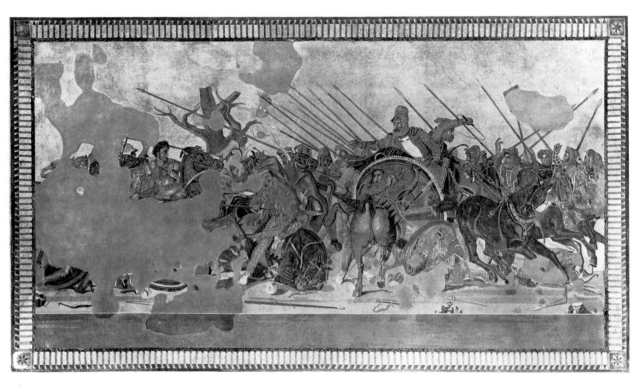

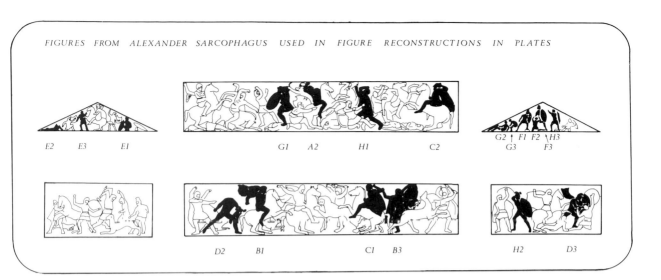

E2   E3   E1

G1   A2   H1   C2

G2 ↑ F1 F2 ↓H3
G3   F3

D2   B1

C1   B3

H2   D3

commanded by Sitalkes, a prince of the Odrysian royal house, and other units may also have been under native commanders. Another unit of javelinmen was commanded by Balacrus.

The Plates

A1: Alexander, uniformed as a senior officer of the Companions

From the Issus mosaic. On the mosaic the tunic and cloak are a light purplish-grey, but the mosaic was copied from an original painting some centuries old, and all the purples had faded by then. The cloak is damaged in the mosaic, but has been reconstructed with a golden-yellow border by comparison with Plate B3. The green girdle worn over the cuirass, and the green edging to the neck-hole of the shabraque may perhaps have some significance as a squadron colour (of the Royal Squadron?). Normally the king would have worn a Boeotian helmet.

A2: Companion cavalryman

From the Alexander Sarcophagus. Normally the Companion would wear a white cuirass, similar to that of Plate A1 but possibly less ornate. Here a Persian saddle cloth is used in place of the Greek saddle (see Plate C1) and the pantherskin shabraque. Presumably the neck-hole of the shabraque and the cuirass girdle would have been in squadron colours.

B1: Companion cavalryman in hunting dress

From a hunting scene on the Alexander Sarcophagus. This Companion has discarded his body armour for the hunt, and has exchanged his *xyston* for a shorter hunting spear. The lining of the shabraque is red in this case—again, perhaps a squadron colour.

B2: Royal page (?) in hunting dress

Based on a mosaic from Pella showing two youths hunting. Other hunting mosaics show similar cloaks, but in plain white, and the huntsmen use the axe and *kopis* (sabre). A white sun hat is worn, not the *kausia*.

B3: Personal Companion in hunting dress

The colours of the cloaks of the Companion Cavalry are reversed in this figure, which is taken from the Alexander Sarcophagus. It is known that Hellenistic kings would give cloaks to their courtiers or 'Friends' as a special mark of favour; so this huntsman is probably one of Alexander's 'Personal' Companions.

C1: Thessalian cavalryman in hunting dress

From a hunting scene on the Alexander Sarcophagus. Only the short-sleeved under-tunic is worn here, the long-sleeved over-tunic being discarded. The shaggy felt saddle cloth is coloured purple and yellow: the purple (of the same dark shade as the cloak) could be the regimental colour of the Thessalians, and the yellow a squadron colour. Note that the harness is medium brown, and not the red which may have been confined to the Companions.

C2: Officer of Thessalian Cavalry
The laurel wreath around the helmet, either painted on or more probably applied in silver, maybe a mark of rank; the same is almost certainly true of the bracelets. The edge of the cloak is obscured on the Sarcophagus, and has been restored as white by comparison with Plate C1. The colours of the cuirass are difficult to determine. Mendel describes it as yellow, but the watercolours of Winter show the *pteruges* as white faced with fine black lines, and this is supported by personal observation and by comparison with Plate A1. The colours of the back-plate are shown as red and white by Winter, but the precise colouration is lost.

D1: Cavalryman of the 'Prodromoi'
Based on a wall painting from the 'Kinch tomb' near Naoussa, This figure shows a light cavalryman in the last years of Philip's reign. Alexander probably replaced the 'Phrygian' helmet with a bronze Boeotian helmet, and substituted a *sarissa* for the *xyston* shown here. The boots and the hem of the tunic are restored. Parts of the helmet are damaged too, but the lappet flowing from under the rim probably belongs to a helmet liner.

D2: Infantryman in camp dress
This figure is loosely based on a figure from a hunting scene on the Alexander Sarcophagus, wearing only a cloak wrapped round his arm. This is the *ephaptis*, the military 'wrap-around' cloak, used by the heavy infantry. This versatile garment, a long, narrow rectangle of cloth, was normally simply draped over the left shoulder, but could be wrapped round the arm to form a makeshift shield if the soldier went hunting, or got into a fight in camp or town. The tunic is restored, as is the *kausia*—its white colour is guesswork, and blue would also be a suitable colour for the infantry. The axe is restored from a mosaic hunting scene at Pella.

D3: Foot Companion in hunting dress
Restored from a half-naked figure in a battle scene on the Sarcophagus. The tunic has been restored in purple, the colour of the *ephaptis* shown on the Sarcophagus; and it allows us to speculate that this

man could be from the same battalion as Plate G2. He is an officer or a senior soldier; the plumes on his helmet are restored.

E1: Hypaspist
From the Alexander Sarcophagus. The upper part of the helmet is obscured in the original, and is restored here. The bronze shield has a deep purple central medallion on the Sarcophagus, but nothing can be made of the device. The boots are similar to those worn by the cavalry.

E2, E3: Unidentified unit (Allied cavalry?)
Both figures come from the Sarcophagus. The helmet of E3 is shown lying behind the figure on the Sarcophagus; that lying next to E2, which is very similar, comes from another scene on the Sarcophagus. The boots worn by both men suggest a cavalry unit, possibly the Allied Horse, but an identification with the Bodyguards is also possible.

F1: Foot Companion
On the Sarcophagus the colours of the shoulder-pieces and the piping on the lower fringe of the groin-flaps are uncertain; and we have also restored the obscured crest of the helmet. The head of Silenos(?) may have been duplicated on a purple background as the shield device of this battalion. The cuirass is not of the standard design; it is richly coloured, but the red tunic does not make us think of an élite battalion.

F2: Greek mercenary in Persian service
He wears a red *exōmis* tunic leaving the right shoulder free, which was normal dress for Greek mercenaries at this time. He has lost his bronze helmet and hoplite shield; this latter would be in plain bronze. Cuirasses were not worn.

F3: Officer of Foot Companions
Based on a figure on the Sarcophagus which seems to represent an officer. The greaves are silvered, and lined with red material to prevent chafing; note also the red garter. The helmet has a gilt spine running along the crest, and plumes, which are restored here. The colours of the shoulder-pieces are uncertain. His shield, shown resting against the wall, is painted with a battalion shield device, the head of an unidentified female deity.

G1: Senior soldier of Foot Companions

From the Sarcophagus; probably a *dekastateros*, *dimoirites*, *dekadarch* or *hyperetes*. The greaves, although indicating a file- or half-file leader, are bronze, not silvered like those of F3. The helmet, though displaying plumes (restored), does not have the gilt spine on the crest. The white spiral painted on the helmet may be the insignia for a *hyperetes*; the 2nd-century tombstone of a *semeiophoros* (standard bearer) of a Ptolemaic infantry unit in Sidon seems to show a similar spiral. The precise outline of this device is uncertain, as the colours have faded; the same is true of the back of the cuirass and the waist belt.

G2: Foot Companion

The purple tunic of this figure, taken from the Sarcophagus, may indicate a soldier of an élite battalion, possibly a battalion of *asthetairoi* or the Elymiotid *taxis* of Coenus.

G3: Servant

On the Sarcophagus the colours of this figure are very faded. The dark purple stripe is fairly certain, but the main ground colour is not: it seems to be a lighter purple similar to that used by the Companion Cavalry, but red is also possible. The status of these servants is unknown, but they may have been Macedonian youths. The ankle-boots are not of standard military type.

H1: Javelinman

No suitable representation of a light infantryman associated with Alexander's army survives. One figure on the Alexander Sarcophagus may possibly be used as a basis for reconstruction, however. He could be a dismounted cavalryman; but if he *is* an infantryman we have to think of him as a light infantryman, for he wears a Macedonian cloak rather than the *ephaptis* of the heavy infantry. The cloak is thrown up over the left shoulder to leave both arms free. Otherwise he is naked: it is possible that the light infantry fought only in cloaks, but the nudity may be a matter of aesthetic presentation, so we have restored a tunic as worn by G3. He may also have worn boots. In the original publication by Hamdy Bey and Reinach (p. 284) the figure is described as striking at the face of a Persian horseman with a javelin, but this is probably a mistake—he seems to be using a sword. The cloak colour is much faded, and could be either a purple of the same shade as that used by the Companions, or red. Purple makes one think of an élite unit—perhaps the Agrianians? The hypothetical nature of all this speculation must be freely admitted.

H2: Unidentified unit (Bodyguard?)

Based on a figure on the Sarcophagus which is shown naked but for helmet and shield. The gilt spine on the helmet, and the plumes (restored), indicate an officer or senior soldier—perhaps greaves and cuirass should also be worn. The tunic could be either purple or red, two-sleeved or an *exōmis*. The shield medallion seems to show Alexander dressed as King of Persia. If this is a regimental shield device, rather than a pure piece of propaganda, it might suggest a unit of Bodyguards or Hypaspists rather than Foot Companions.

H3: Allied Greek infantryman

Based on a figure on the Sarcophagus. The shield would have been plain bronze, but may have been painted with the device of the city in which the detachment was raised. The warrior is shown bareheaded apart from a head-band, but his helmet is shown lying at his feet.

Further Reading

Two modern accounts of Alexander's reign, both well-written and generally available, are *Alexander the Great* by Robin Lane Fox (Allan Lane 1973, Omega Books 1975, 1978) and *Alexander of Macedon* by Peter Green (Penguin 1974). Philip's army is dealt with in Chapter XII of *A History of Macedonia, Volume II* by N. G. L. Hammond and G. T. Griffith (Clarendon Press, Oxford 1979). The standard treatment of the use Alexander made of his army is still J. F. C. Fuller's *The Generalship of Alexander the Great* (London 1958), but E. W. Marsden's *The Campaign of Gaugamela* (Liverpool University Press 1964) has added a lot to our knowledge of Alexander's principal campaign. Donald W. Engels' *Alexander the Great and the Logistics of the Macedonian Army* (University of California Press 1978) deals with questions of supply. A good introduction to military dress and equipment during this period and later is given by Duncan Head's *Armies of the Macedonian and Punic Wars*

(Wargames Research Group 1982).

Plutarch's *The Age of Alexander* and Arrian's *The Campaigns of Alexander* are both currently available in Penguin Classics, but anyone wishing to make a detailed study of Alexander's army will eventually be forced to use translations giving the Greek text in parallel. Most of the ancient sources used in this book are available in this form in the 'Loeb Classical Library' Series published jointly by William Heinemann Ltd. and Harvard University Press. Volume 1 of P. A. Brunt's translation of Arrian contains an introduction with many useful notes. The only English translation of Polyaenus currently available (to my knowledge) is the 1793 translation of R. Shepherd, available in reprint from Ares Publishers Inc. (Chicago 1974).

There are some hundreds of scholarly articles concerning various aspects of Alexander's army— too many to list here. Fortunately, though, two commentaries have recently been published covering Arrian and Curtius. Readers wishing to follow the debate in that depth will be able to find further references in these works, which are *A Historical Commentary on Arrian's History of Alexander, Volume I* by A. B. Bosworth (Clarendon Press, Oxford 1980) and *A Commentary on Q. Curtius Rufus' Historiae Alexandri Magni, Books 3 and 4* by J. E. Atkinson (J. C. Gieben, Amsterdam 1980).

Notes sur les planches en couleur

A1 On peut voir sur la mosaïque d'Issus un vêtement de couleur gris-pourpre clair qui était peut-être à l'origine d'un ton plus foncé qu'il n'est maintenant. La ceinture verte et l'ornement vert sur la *shabraque* peuvent être des signes distinctifs identifiant l'Escadron Royal. **A2** Il porterait normalement une cuirasse blanche, comme A1, mais peut-être moins chargée d'ornements. Un tapis de selle perse remplace ici la selle et la peau de panthère *shabraque* grecques qui étaient vraisemblablement normales.

B1 Ce personnage est une reconstruction d'après le sarcophage d'Alexandre à Istanbul, comme presque tous les personnages de ces gravures. La doublure rouge de la *shabraque* pourrait être une marque d'identification d'un escadron du régiment. **B2** Cette reproduction est basée sur une mosaïque à Pella: remarquez le chapeau blanc protégeant du soleil. **B3** Les couleurs de l'uniforme du Régiment de Cavalerie des Compagnons sont inversées ici: couleur or pour le pourpre. D'après notre connaissance des coutumes du monde hellénistique il pourrait s'agir d'un manteau offert par le roi à ses courtisans favoris, ce qui permettrait donc d'identifier les 'Compagnons Personnels'.

C1 On a supprimé la tunique de dessus aux manches longues. Le tapis de selle de couleur pourpre foncée pourrait identifier les Thessaliens. **C2** Le torque sur le casque, peint ou en argent fin appliqué, ainsi que les bracelets portés sur les bras sont très certainement des signes distinctifs de grade.

D1 Ce cavalier, d'après une peinture murale de la tombe dite '*Kinch*' près de Naoussa, est probablement identifié par sa barbe pleine et son casque phrygien comme datant du règne de Philippe: Alexandre a introduit le casque béotien et le rasage de frais. **D2** L'*ephaptis*, ou manteau militaire de l'infanterie lourde pouvait servir à envelopper le bras en guise de bouclier de fortune lors de chasses ou de bagarres. La parure de tête *kausia*, caractéristique des Macédoniens, pouvait peut-être être blanche ou bleue pour l'infanterie. **D3** Le plumet du casque indique qu'il s'agit d'un officier ou d'un sous-officier. La tunique pourpre pourrait indiquer qu'il s'agit d'un soldat appartenant à la même unité que celui de la gravure G2.

E1 On peut voir sur le sarcophage un bouclier de bronze portant au centre un médaillon de couleur pourpre foncée, cependant le dessin exact peint sur ce médaillon n'est pas identifiable. Il n'était pas rare de faire figurer des représentations de divinités. **E2, E3** Les bottes suggèrent qu'il s'agit de cavaliers appartenant peut-être au Cheval Allié, ou aux Gardes du Corps.

F1 Il se peut que la face de Silenos (?) sur ce bouclier soit un signe distinctif de bataillon. La tunique rouge tend à suggérer que ce serait une unité de moindre statut que l'élite. **F2** L'*exomis* rouge est caractéristique des mercenaires grecs de cette période. Ils portaient généralement un casque de bronze et un bouclier de bronze sans ornements, mais n'avaient pas de cuirasse. **F3** D'après les jambières argentées, le plumet du casque et le cimier du casque doré il s'agirait d'un officier.

G1 Les jambières sont en bronze, le casque est dépourvu de cimier doré mais a un dessin en forme de spirale. D'après la comparaison d'un personnage figurant sur le sarcophage à celui d'une tombe datant d'une époque plus récente et située à Sidon, ce pourrait être un soldat de grade supérieur, un chef de colonne ou de demi-colonne. **G2** La tunique pourpre indique peut-être qu'il s'agit d'un bataillon d'élite. **G3** Reconstruction expérimentale d'après un personnage du sarcophage dont les couleurs se sont très estompées.

H1 Reconstruction hypothétique d'après un personnage du sarcophage aux couleurs passées, sur lequel on peut cependant voir clairement le style macédonien du manteau plutôt que l'*ephaptis*. **H2** L'emblème du bouclier semble représenter Alexandre comme Roi de Perse Si cet emblème est celui d'une unité, ce pourrait être une unité de Gardes du Corps ou *Hypaspists* plutôt que des Compagnons à Pied. **H3** Il se pourrait qu'il y ait eu une lettre d'initiale ou un autre dessin propre à la cité où l'unité fut recrutée sur ce bouclier de bronze lisse.

Farbtafeln

A1 Das Issus Mosaik zeigt helle, purpurgraue Kleidung, ursprünlich vielleicht von stärkerer Farbe als heute sichtbar. Der grüne Gürtel und der Besatz auf der 'shabraque' bezeichnen möglicherweise das Königliche Schwadron. **A2** Normalerweise würde hier ein weisser Kürass getragen, vielleicht weniger geschmückt als bei A1. Hier sind die vermutlich normale griechische Satteldecke und die 'shabraque' aus Pantherhaut durch eine persische Satteldecke ersetzt.

B1 Wie fast alle Figuren auf diesen Tafeln ist auch diese hier nach dem Alexander-Sarkophag in Istanbul rekonstruiert. Der rote Stoff auf der 'shabraque' könnte ein Schwadron innerhalb des Regiments identifizieren. **B2** Aus einem Mosaik in Pella; man beachte den weissen Sonnenhut. **B3** Die Uniformfarben des Gefährten-Kavallerieregiments sind hier umgekehrt—gold für purpur. Die heute noch bekannten Gebräuche der hellenistischen Welt lassen sich hier nahe, dass es sich um einen vom König an einen favorisierten Höfling geschenkten Mantel handeln könnte, der vielleicht die 'Persönlichen Gefährten' auszeichnete.

C1 Die langärmlige obere Tunika ist abgelegt. Die tiefpurpurne Satteldecke bezeichnete vielleicht die Thessalier. **C2** Der entweder aufgemalte oder in dünner Silberschmiedearbeit aufgesetzte Kranz auf dem Helm und die Armreife sind zweifellos Rangabzeichen.

D1 Aus einer Wandmalerei des sogenannten 'Kinch-Grabes' inder Nähe von Naoussa. Dieser leichte Kavallerist lässt sich durch seinen Vollbart und den phrygischen Helm vermutlich in die Regierungszeit Philipps; Alexander führte den boötischen Helm ein und liess seine Soldaten sich glatt rasieren. **D2** Der 'ephaptis', der Militärmantel der schweren Infanterie, konnte bei der Jagd oder bei Streitigkeiten um den Arm gewickelt und anstelle eines Schildes benutzt werden. Der für die Mazedonier typische 'kausia' Kopfputz wurde vermutlich in weiss oder von der Infanterie in blau getragen. **D3** Die Helmfedern bezeichnen einen Offizier oder leitenden Unteroffizier. Die purpurne Tunika weist vielleicht ein Mitglied derselben Einheit wie bei Tafel G2 aus.

E1 Der Sarkophag zeigt einen Bronzeschild mit dunkel purpurnem Medaillon in der Mitte, die genaue Abbildung ist unklar. Darstellungen von Gottheiten waren nicht ungewöhnlich. **E2, E3** Die Stiefel weisen auf Kavalleristen hin, vielleicht von den Vereinigten Pferdetruppen, aber es könnte sich auch um Leibwächter handeln.

F1 Silenuskopf (?) auf dem Schild, vielleicht ein Schlachtenabzeichen. Die rote Tunika verweist auf eine Einheit von geringerer Bedeutung. **F2** Der rote 'exomis' ist typisch für griechische Söldner dieser Zeit. Der Söldner trug normalerweise einen Bronzehelm und einen Bronzeschild ohne allegorische Darstellungen, aber keinen Kürass. **F3** Die versilberten Beinschienen, Helmfedern und der vergoldete Helmschmuck verweisen auf einen Offizier.

G1 Die Beinschienen sind aus Bronze; der Helm hat keinen vergoldeten Helmschmuck, aber ein spiralförmiges Abzeichen. Ein Vergleich einer Figur auf dem Sarkophag und einer anderen auf einem späteren Grabstein in Sidon deuten auf einen leitenden Unteroffizier, einen Rotten- oder Halbrottenführer hin. **G2** Die purpurne Tunika verweist auf einen Elitebataillon. **G3** Vorsichtige Rekonstruktion einer stark verblassten Figur auf dem Sarkophag.

H1 Hypothetische Rekonstruktion einer stark verblassten Figur auf dem Sarkophag, auf dem allerdings der Mantel im mazedonischen Stil anstelle der 'ephaptis' zu erkennen ist. **H2** Auf dem Schild ist anscheinend Alexander als König von Persien abgebildet. Falls es sich um ein Einheitsabzeichen handelt, liegt eine Einheit von Leibwächtern oder 'Hypaspists' näher als eine Infanterieeinheit. **H3** Der einfache Bronzeschild trug vielleicht den Anfangsbuchstaben oder ein Wappen der Stadt, in der die Einheit ausgehoben wurde.